Club Management

The management of private membership clubs

Clayton Barrows

and

Michael Robinson

with illustrations by

John Klossner

(G) Goodfellow Publishers Ltd

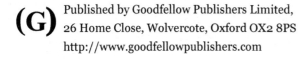 Published by Goodfellow Publishers Limited,
26 Home Close, Wolvercote, Oxford OX2 8PS
http://www.goodfellowpublishers.com

British Library Cataloguing in Publication Data: a catalogue
record for this title is available from the British Library.

Library of Congress Catalog Card Number: on file.

ISBN: 978-1-911635-06-2

 Design and typesetting by P.K. McBride, www.macbride.org.uk

Cover design by Cylinder

Printed by Baker & Taylor, www.baker-taylor.com

Contents

Acknowledgments

Assembling the information for this club management text has been an education, to say the least. A good amount of the historical information was gleaned from references developed by earlier researchers. Many of the dates that appear are based on the best available information and may be challenged by still other researchers of club history. We learned that not all dates are etched in stone.

What is readily apparent is that there are a large number of educators, practitioners, vendors, historians, clubs, associations, publications and students that are stakeholders in the operation of clubs and club management in particular.

During our journey we have been assisted by numerous phone conversations, visits with managers at clubs, in-person interviews, library discoveries, information shared at national conferences, talks with other educators, and symposiums and roundtables, and through social media. We have spoken with professionals in almost all of the club management disciplines. The outreach has been genuine and heartfelt. Thank you all for your generous participation, your comments and selfless contributions. We could not have done it without you.

Finally, thank you the publisher, for allowing us to use this canvas to share information and insights on the club management profession with fellow stakeholders.

Clayton W. Barrows, Greenland, New Hampshire

Michael Robinson, Saint Augustine, Florida

1 Introduction to Clubs

Private clubs have existed for as long as people have desired to gather in groups to do things together. It has been suggested that private clubs (and their predecessors) date to the Roman baths but probably pre-date even those. It is doubtful that the Roman baths represented the first time people congregated in groups to socialize, discuss commerce, politics, or just engage in a mutually agreeable activity.

Certainly, most agree that the 'modern' clubs (in the English speaking world) originated in England, were limited to 'gentlemen' and organized for social, political, business and/or pleasure reasons. The concept was then 'exported' along with ex-patriots all around the world. Clubs have since evolved to the point where they exist in countries around the world although they are embraced to a greater or lesser extent in different places. Examples of private clubs can be found in such countries as England (and the greater UK), Ireland, the United States, Canada, Australia and New Zealand, South Africa, Switzerland, Hong Kong, India, Pakistan, Japan, Singapore, and the UAE. Perhaps no country has adopted the idea of clubs as much as the USA, where they have evolved into a veritable industry, are protected by law, and number into the thousands.

Humans, being social creatures, long to spend quality time with others – 'others', historically, representing those of their own kind. Perhaps it is for this reason that clubs have, rightly or wrongly, developed a reputation for being discriminatory. People generally find benefits from spending time with others. These benefits may accrue in many forms, including personal, professional, and political.

While much of the hospitality industry is defined and characterized by its offering 'public accommodation', to willing, paying customers, clubs are different. Clubs exist to serve a limited membership. They are, by definition, limited to members only. This is true, even though the word 'club' is often used indiscriminately. There is no rule governing how the word is used but suffice it to say that not all organizations or businesses that use the word to describe themselves, are clubs by our definition. A true club is premised on a selective membership and there is a process of admission (which will be discussed later). However, it is important to know that membership is selective and may be based on a number of factors, including one's personal and professional connections, one's social standing, and one's character, as well as one's ability to pay.

Photo 1.1: Manchester Country Club, by Gil Talbot Photography, courtesy of Manchester Country Club, (Manchester, New Hampshire, USA).

At this point, it is worth reiterating that clubs are different from other types of hospitality organizations, or public accommodations. They are governed by different rules, different laws and they exist to serve a different clientele. It also means that they have a different set of objectives as well as challenges. But first, more about what clubs are.

The most common type of club with which most students will be familiar is the country club, which focuses on golf as its primary activity but also offers a myriad of other activities. Perhaps students are familiar with this type of club already having worked at one, grown up as a member, or visited one with a friend or relative. Country clubs are the most popular, most common and most visible type of club in much of the world. One of the purposes of this book though is to explore some of the other types of clubs, which often receive less attention.

The history of the Old Colony Club (Exhibit 1.1) provides several lessons for students of the club industry. It is representative of all clubs, in that it started as a gathering of like-minded individuals with mutual interests; it went through some tough times which resulted in its dissolution; politics played a key role in its early days; and it highlights the important role that tradition plays in all clubs.

Exhibit 1.1: Profile of Old Colony Club

One of the more interesting clubs that we have encountered, and one with direct ties to early American roots, is the Old Colony Club in Plymouth, Massachusetts. It was founded in 1769 by a small group of individuals, many of whom were direct descendants of Mayflower passengers. It was originally established to (among other reasons) " … avoid the many disadvantages and inconveniences that arise from intermixing with the company at the taverns in this town." The club allowed its members to socialize amongst themselves, and to enhance their general happiness. Membership also allowed them to debate the attributes of the Tories and the Whigs (early American political parties). Much of their purpose was also established on observing and celebrating Forefathers' Day (an observance that continues to today). Unfortunately, the political debates proved to be too much, resulting in the departure of the Loyalist members. This resulted in the closing of the club in 1773. However, it was reformed in 1875 wherein discussions of politics were forbidden:

"Gambling, intoxicating liquor, public demonstrations for political parties, partisan political discussion, and loud and boisterous talk were forbidden."

Over the years, the club was organized, reorganized (1883) and moved several times. It moved in 1893 into its current location, where members continue to get together for social occasions and to celebrate the founding of the country. An excellent account of their history can be found at http:// www.oldcolonyclub.org.

We will profile many different clubs throughout this book. Students should attempt to identify commonalities and differences amongst and between the different clubs.

We have begun to describe what clubs are but it should be made clear that clubs differ from every other segment of the hospitality industry in many ways: perhaps the most significant factor that sets them apart, from a management perspective, is the privacy element which limits the enjoyment of its products and services to members only.

Other factors which set them apart also include the:

- Product and service mix that they offer
- Quality of services offered
- Facilities
- Ownership

- Governance
- Management structures and how decisions get made
- Finances
- Food and beverage model
- Organizational objectives
- History and traditions
- Role of the general manager

Introduction

Each of these will be discussed in turn. Perhaps the factor that most sets them apart from other hospitality sectors is the fact that each club is unique: that is to say, no two clubs are exactly alike. This is true even for 'chains' of clubs, such as those operated by ClubCorp, ClubLink (Canada), Signature Clubs International, KemperSports or Troon Privé. While the policies and procedures at these affiliated clubs may be the same from club to club, the members, culture, activities, traditions and physical environment differ. The same thing cannot be said of chain operations in other hospitality sectors where, in fact, the goal is to achieve a certain level of sameness. Clubs pride themselves on their own distinctness, something that can give their members bragging rights.

Before proceeding, we would like to profile a unique club, located in Calgary, Alberta, Canada to prove our point.

Exhibit 1.2: The Ranchmen's Club

The Ranchmen's Club is located in downtown Calgary, Alberta (Canada). It has a long and colourful history, having been established in 1891 by a group of (primarily) cattlemen. In fact, the club just celebrated its 125th anniversary. According to former general manager, David Houghton, early meetings of its founders were held in a railway car, before moving into a more permanent location. By 1907, the club had approximately 80 members whose primary activities were eating, drinking, reading and socializing, and the club moved into a new clubhouse in 1914. As the cattle industry in Calgary changed, the club also changed. Today, the club has over 1,000 members from diverse professions, who enjoy a variety a dining options, social events and a private art collection. The club is located in a downtown area and thus, would be classified as a 'city club'. Many city clubs also offer athletic activities. While The Ranchmen's Club does not have any athletic facilities of its own, its members are able to enjoy golf at three local courses as well as being able to use the facilities at a local athletic club. Perhaps the most interesting aspect of the club though is its arts program. Jim McLeod, former president of the club, describes it this way.

"Since the turn of the twentieth century, the Ranchmen's Club has collected artwork from time to time and in 2006 it formed the Heritage & Art Sub-Committee to administer the Art Collection, including acquisitions, deaccessions, care/maintenance, inventory and, education/events. The Sub-Committee is volunteer based; has a Chair and Vice-Chair; currently comprises about 20 Club Members and, two staff; and, reports to the Committee of Management ('Board'). The Sub-Committee meets monthly. From time to time the Sub-Committee will host art education themed receptions and dinners – two to four per year – and the Annual Emerging Artist event each spring which features 30-35 up and coming artists from the City of Calgary and vicinity. The Clubs' Collection numbers about 150 historic to contemporary paintings and sculptures by noted Canadian artists. The artwork is displayed throughout the Clubs' premises and each item is meticulously catalogued – provenance, etc. – and a placard mounted nearby each piece detailing the artist, medium, title, etc. The Sub-Committee is also responsible for administering the Clubs' Library – historic books and art related books, antiques, furniture, etc. – and archival records."

The authors are often asked what it is that prompts our personal and professional interest in clubs. In addition to having enjoyed our respective professional careers in the industry (one short and one quite long), we answer that clubs combine all of the best elements of hospitality, are service driven, offer great job prospects for our students, are pleasant place to work, and are interesting! But before we continue, we should properly define what club is.

What is a club?

What do we mean when we talk about clubs? We are talking about formal organizations where people of similar interests congregate for a variety of purposes (golf or dining or tennis or sailing, etc.). These organizations are of a certain size, such that they are recognized by the government as legal entities; are of a certain critical mass so as to require formal organization; have a financial base; have a physical facility; offer certain products and services; are private (members only); and require the management expertise of a dedicated executive who looks after day to day responsibilities. Not included in this discussion are nightclubs, fraternities and sororities, health 'clubs' (such as

Planet Fitness), Boy Scouts/Girls Guides, business organizations, lobbying groups, book clubs, student organizations, or academic associations. While each of these may have certain characteristics which are similar to those of private clubs, none serves the exact same purpose as a private club nor do they function as such.

Some well-known examples of private clubs include The Royal and Ancient (St Andrews, Scotland), The Country Club (USA), Augusta National, Pinehurst, Pebble Beach, the Tokyo American Club (Japan), Capital Club (Dubai) and the Royal Calcutta Golf Club (India). These clubs generally conjure up images of being exclusive, expensive, and prestigious– which they generally are. Some cost several hundred thousand dollars to join.

One of the best definitions of clubs was set forth in 1895 and still effectively describes clubs of today. From Wertheimer's *Law Relating to Clubs*:

"A CLUB may be defined to be a voluntary association of a number of persons meeting together for purposes mainly social, each contributing a certain sum either to a common fund for the benefit of the members or to a particular individual for his own benefit. Where the contributions are paid to a common fund the society is a members' club (a), where to a particular individual it is a proprietary club. Those clubs which are distinguished by the title 'West-end clubs' were described by the late Lord Romilly, M.R., as "very peculiar institutions. They are societies of gentlemen who meet principally for social purposes, superadded to which there are often certain other purposes, sometimes of a literary nature, sometimes to promote political objects, as in the Conservative or the Reform Club. But the principal objects for which they are designed are social, the others are only secondary"
(b). A club, as a body, has no position recognized in law (c), and although frequently confounded with other voluntary associations, it is really an institution."

In short, clubs (at least member-owned clubs) exist to allow their members social and recreational opportunities without a profit motive. While this refers primarily to not-for-profit clubs, keep in mind that some clubs operate to make a profit (identified as 'proprietary clubs' above).

The definition of a club is still largely driven by the government and accompanying legal restrictions. For instance, in the USA, one type of club (not-for-profit, or 501 (c) 7) must satisfy the restrictions as dictated by the Internal Revenue Service (IRS) which states how they are organized, what their mission is, and how they are treated. This is presented in Exhibit 1.3.

The government looks at several criteria in order to determine that a club is actually a club, including but not limited to: its size; exclusiveness; selectivity of membership; use of facilities; member governance; and criteria for membership. Clubs must satisfy these standards (at least in the USA) if they are to maintain tax exemption and exemption from other laws (such as the Civil Rights Act, Title II, which prohibits discrimination).

Exhibit 1.3:
IRS Definition of a Nonprofit Private Club

501(c) (7) - Social and Recreation Clubs

If your club is organized for pleasure, recreation, and other similar nonprofitable purposes and substantially all of its activities are for these purposes, it should file Form 1024 to apply for recognition of exemption from federal income tax.

In applying for recognition of exemption, you should submit the information described in this section. Also see Chapter 1 for the procedures to follow.

Typical organizations that should file for recognition of exemption as social clubs include:

■ College alumni associations that are not described in Chapter 3 under _Alumni association_

■ College fraternities or sororities operating chapter houses for students,

■ Country clubs,

■ Amateur hunting, fishing, tennis, swimming, and other sport clubs,

■ Dinner clubs that provide a meeting place, library, and dining room for members,

■ Hobby clubs,

■ Garden clubs, and

■ Variety clubs.

Discrimination prohibited

Your organization will not be recognized as tax exempt if its charter, bylaws, or other governing instrument, or any written policy statement provides for discrimination against any person on the basis of race, color, or religion.

However, a club that in good faith limits its membership to the members of a particular religion to further the teachings or principles of that religion and not to exclude individuals of a particular race or color will not be considered as discriminating on the basis of religion. Also, the restriction on religious discrimination does not apply to a club that is an auxiliary of a fraternal beneficiary society (discussed later) if that society is described in section 501(c)(8) and exempt from tax under section 501(a) and limits its membership to the members of a particular religion.

Private benefit prohibited

No part of the organization's net earnings can inure to the benefit of any person having a personal and private interest in the activities of the organization. For purposes of this requirement, it is not necessary that net earnings be actually distributed. Even undistributed earnings can benefit members. Examples of this include a decrease in membership dues or an increase in the services the club provides to its members without a corresponding increase in dues or other fees paid for club support. However, fixed-fee payments to members who bring new members into the club are not an inurement of the club's net earnings, if the payments are reasonable compensation for performance of a necessary administrative service.

Purposes

To show that your organization possesses the characteristics of a club within the meaning of the exemption law, you should submit evidence with your application that personal contact, commingling, and fellowship exist among members. You must show that members are bound together by a common objective of pleasure, recreation, and other nonprofitable purposes.

Fellowship need not be present between each member and every other member of a club if it is a material part in the life of the organization. A statewide or nationwide organization that is made up of individual members, but is divided into local groups, satisfies this requirement if fellowship is a material part of the life of each local group.   The term 'other nonprofitable purposes' means other purposes similar to pleasure and recreation. For example, a club that, in addition to its social activities, has a plan for the payment of sick and death benefits is not operating exclusively for pleasure, recreation, and other nonprofitable purposes.

Limited membership.

The membership in a social club must be limited. To show that your organization has a purpose that would characterize it as a club, you should submit evidence with your application that there are limits on admission to membership consistent with the character of the club.

A social club that issues corporate membership is dealing with the general public in the form of the corporation's employees. Corporate members of a club are not the kind of members contemplated by the law. Gross receipts from these members would be a factor in determining whether the club qualifies as a social club. See *Gross receipts from nonmembership sources*, later. Bona fide individual memberships paid for by a corporation would not have an effect on the gross receipts source. The fact that a social club may have an associate (nonvoting) class of membership will not be, in and of itself, a cause for nonrecognition of exemption. However, if one membership class pays substantially lower dues and fees than another membership class, although both classes enjoy the same rights and privileges in using the club facilities, there may be an inurement of income to the benefited class, resulting in a denial of the club's exemption.

Support

In general, your club should be supported solely by membership fees, dues, and assessments. However, if otherwise entitled to exemption, your club will not be disqualified because it raises revenue from members through the use of club facilities or in connection with club activities.

Business activities

If your club will engage in business, such as selling real estate, timber, or other products or services, it generally will be denied exemption. However, evidence submitted with your application form that your organization will provide meals, refreshments, or services related to its exempt purposes only to its own members or their dependents or guests will not cause denial of exemption.

Facilities open to public

Evidence that your club's facilities will be open to the general public (persons other than members or their dependents or guests) may cause denial of exemption. This does not mean, however, that any dealing with outsiders will automatically deprive a club of exemption.

Gross receipts from nonmembership sources.

A section 501(c)(7) organization can receive up to 35% of its gross receipts, including investment income, from sources outside of its membership without losing its tax-exempt status. Income from nontraditional business activity with members is not exempt function income, and thus is included as income from sources outside of the membership. Of the 35% gross receipts listed above, up to 15% of the gross receipts can be derived from the use of the club's facilities or services by the general public. If an organization has outside income that is more than these limits, all the facts and circumstances will be taken into account in determining whether the organization qualifies for exempt status.

Gross receipts

Gross receipts, for this purpose, are receipts from the normal and usual (traditionally conducted) activities of the club. These receipts include charges, admissions, membership fees, dues, assessments, investment income, and normal recurring capital gains on investments. Receipts do not include initiation fees and capital contributions. Unusual amounts of income, such as from the sale of a clubhouse or similar facility, are not included in gross receipts or in figuring the percentage limits.

Nontraditional activities

Activities conducted by a social club need to further its exempt purposes. Traditional business activities are those that further a social club's exempt purposes. Nontraditional business activities do not further the exempt purposes of a social club even if conducted solely on a membership basis. Nontraditional business activities are prohibited (subject to an insubstantial, trivial, and nonrecurrent test) for businesses conducted with both members and nonmembers. Examples of nontraditional business activities include sale of package liquor, take-out food, and long-term room rental.

Fraternity foundations

If your organization is a foundation formed for the exclusive purpose of acquiring and leasing a chapter house to a local fraternity chapter or sorority chapter maintained at an educational institution and does not engage in any social or recreational activities, it may be a title holding corporation (discussed later under section 501(c)(2) organizations and under section 501(c)(25) organizations) rather than a social club.

Tax treatment of donations

Donations to exempt social and recreation clubs are not deductible as charitable contributions on the donor's federal income tax return.

Source: From the Internal Revenue Service (https://www.irs.gov/publications/p557/ch04. html#en_US_201502_publink1000200325)

Clubs take many forms. There are so many different types of clubs offering so many different types of activities that as soon as one begins to try to classify them, many defy classification. For instance, there are golf clubs that offer hunting; yacht clubs that have golf; and canoe clubs that do not offer canoeing! One of the most interesting clubs that we have seen was situated in a city, on a lake (but did not offer yachting or swimming), offered multiple recreational activities (but no golf) and, of course, dining. It did not fit any of our pre-conceived notions of a particular type of club (not a city club, not a yacht club and not a country club).

Typically though, clubs are classified on the basis of their primary activity, be it golf, tennis, yachting (sailing), skiing, etc. In this vein, they may also be classified on the basis of their location (e.g. city or country). When these terms are used though, it is generally understood that a 'country' club offers golf and other activities while 'city' clubs offer food and beverage, rooms (sometimes) and athletics (sometimes).

The point is, every club offers its own unique combination of services and activities – a mix that has probably changed over time as their member preferences have changed. However, we will try to describe the most common types of clubs here.

- **Golf and country clubs:** Many clubs offer golf and other activities. Those that offer golf as their primary activity are referred to as golf clubs. Those that offer golf in addition to other recreational activities (such as tennis and swimming) are usually referred to as country clubs. Clubs that focus on one primary recreational activity are usually referred to after that activity: tennis (or racquet); hunt; yacht; etc.

- **City clubs** typically offer food and beverage services and many offer one or more recreational activities such as squash or fitness. Many city clubs also have guest rooms. For instance, the Union League Club (Chicago), established in 1879, offers multiple food and beverage outlets, extensive athletic facilities (pool, squash, fitness, etc.) and 180 guest rooms. Most city clubs are not this large however. Some simply offer dining while others offer a whole range of facilities and activities.

- **University clubs** are a specific type of city club that cater to the graduates of a particular university (while some offer admission to graduates of any university). Well known examples include those affiliated with Ivy League schools, such as the Yale Club, the Princeton Club and the Harvard Club. In fact, the Harvard Club has multiple locations including New York and Boston. With all of these, the common bond for members is, obviously, the school that they attended.

  Other university clubs may be unaffiliated with a particular college or university. For instance, there is the University Club of Boston, the University Club of New York, and the University Club of Chicago, among others. Many of these clubs simply require that members possess a college or university degree, rather than a degree from a specific school. University clubs are typically located in downtown locations, offer similar services to that of other city clubs, and, often, overnight rooms.

- **Arts and letters** (or arts and literature) clubs also also tend to be located in city centres, and cater to artists, writers and musicians, and others dedicated to the arts. They often have readings, art exhibits and musical performances.

One such example is the Arts and Letters Club in Toronto (founded in 1908) whose purpose "was to be a rendezvous where people of diverse interests might meet for mutual fellowship and artistic creativity."

- **Hunt clubs** still exist where hunting is permissible (hunting has been severely restricted and/or banned in many areas thus forcing hunt clubs to seek alternative missions). As a result, hunt clubs represent one type of club that has gone through extreme changes in the last 100 years. Some of today's well-known country clubs started as hunt clubs and then changed over time to adopt new forms of recreation.

- **Yacht clubs** are located near water (lakes or oceans) and offer yachting (usually sailing) to their members. Members have the common interest of boating (or sailing) and other activities may be limited. 'Regattas' tend to be a primary event at such clubs.

These are some of the more common clubs. Clubs may be organized around virtually any activity or interest though. And often they combine activities, which will be shown. Different types of clubs and way of classifying them will be discussed in greater detail in Chapter 2.

Before we proceed, let's try to visualize what a 'typical' club might look like. A club can have anywhere from a few members to thousands (we know of one club in Canada with 10,000 members). It will have one (or two) primary activities, such as golf or dining or sailing. It will also typically offer food and beverage and, in fact, some clubs offer so many dining operations, they are more like large hotels. This 'typical' club will be housed in a stately building (if it is in the city) or on expansive grounds, if it encompasses outdoor sports. More specific examples of each type of club will be given in the next chapter.

Profile of the industry

Nobody is quite sure how large the industry is. One reason for this is that different types of clubs are classified by the government into different types of business categories. In the USA, the Internal Revenue Service (tax authority in the USA) also classifies them on the basis of their being run as for-profit or not-for-profit. Some estimates suggest that there are upwards of 15,000 private clubs in the USA. Perhaps the best proxy is the number of member clubs in the professional club associations. For instance, 2,500 clubs are represented in the *Club Management Association of America* but one cannot be sure of how many clubs this represents of the total.

We do know that clubs are widely dispersed across states and provinces, regions, countries and continents. We also know that many had their origins around archery, hunting, polo, horseback riding, and eventually, golf. Despite their common origins, traditions vary across countries and cultures. We will give some examples as we discuss some of the early clubs.

As we progress with our discussion of clubs, you will note that they are currently going through many changes. As we tell our students, clubs did not change much for 100 (or more) years and then have undergone extensive changes just in the last 10 to 20 years. But before we embark on the current status of clubs, a review of their history is in order.

Please note that because clubs' origins are often sketchy given their long histories and (sometimes) lost records. Also, clubs close, burn down or move; may operate without an official charter for a time before officially organizing and gaining a charter; and others merge with other clubs. As a result, it can often be challenging to definitively state when and where a club officially began. However, the following is based upon reliable documentation.

History of clubs

As noted above, it is almost impossible to determine the first time that the concept of a 'club' first originated. Instead of trying to identify their origins, we will discuss the early history of clubs in the UK, Canada, India and the USA.

City clubs

City clubs (or gentlemen's clubs) preceded golf clubs in the UK and elsewhere. Early clubs in the UK centred around London and evolved from the coffee houses – they typically were comprised of groups of men who paid a small admittance fee for the privilege of drinking coffee, reading the local newspapers and playing cards. These groups eventually became more formalized, developed by-laws of sorts, and moved to private rooms in these same coffee houses. Eventually, they moved off site and incorporated.

Photo 1.2: The Byculla Club, Courtesy of the British Library

White's is generally regarded as being the first of the London gentlemen's clubs and actually started at White's Chocolate House as 'The Club at White's'. It began in 1693 (or perhaps 1697) but regardless is now over 300 years old. Its history is well documented in two books, most recently in *White's: The First Three-Hundred Years*. The club is now located in the St. James's area of London, known as 'Clubland'. Early records indicate there were 82 members at the formation of the club. John James Heidegger was an original member, who put on masquerade balls for members. Over the years, White's had such honourable members as various prime ministers, statesmen, military officers, etc.

The original chocolate house was owned and operated by Francis White and carried on after his death by, first, his wife and then son. The history of White's coincides with the fascinating introduction of first, chocolate, and then coffee, to London. Bourke has suggested that early coffee houses were "the only means of the expression of public opinion." White's offered this and more as eating, drinking and gambling seemed to be popular activities. The original White's burned down in 1733 and moved once and then three more times, finally to its current location.

Other early city club in London include Boodle's (1762) and Brook's (1764), both of which continue to operate today.

City clubs in North America

City clubs in the USA started in the northeastern part of the country, in Massachusetts, New York and Pennsylvania (specifically, Philadelphia). Early clubs included the Old Colony Club in Plymouth, Massachusetts (established in 1769). Although it was and is primarily a social club and not in a major city, it is mentioned here. It is considered the oldest social club in the USA, and is profiled in Exhibit 1.1.

The Philadelphia Club (established in 1834) can be considered the oldest continuously operating city club in the USA (although it was first known as the Adelphi Club). It began with members meeting at Rubicam's Coffee House. It is still in operation and has been in its current location since 1850. Similar to the clubs of London in the previous century, the Philadelphia Club began when two independent groups of friends began to gather at Rubicam's Coffee House and also at Arney's Coffee House. They joined forces in 1834, moved to the Adelphi building in 1834 and moved again and changed their name in 1835. Article 1 from their bylaws states: "This club shall be termed the 'Philadelphia Club' and its object shall be the encouragement of social intercourse (Wister, p. 14.)" Early activities included cards, billiards and other games. The club originally provided a reading room and a dining room and later offered overnight guest rooms. When it was first founded, it had 62 members and charged an initiation fee of $40.00. The origins, size, exclusivity, by-laws and statement of purpose were all elements that can be found in other clubs established later in the century.

Canada also has a long history of city clubs. Perhaps the earliest was the Beaver Club, which was established in 1785. It was small, exclusive, and based in Montreal. Its members were all associated with the North West Company, which focused on fur trading. It had a short, but lively existence, having disbanded in 1824.

Following the Beaver Club, the earliest club (that is still in existence) is the Toronto Club (established in 1837). The Toronto Club moved several times in its early years but was housed in the British Coffee House (twice), again reflecting the historic connection between clubs and coffee houses, before moving to its current location in 1889.

Within just a two-three year period, the Philadelphia Club, Toronto Club and then the Union Club (of New York, 1836) were all established (the latter club had (with antecedents dating back to 1822).) and then the Toronto Club were all established. A profile of the University Club of St. Louis is presented in Exhibit 1.4.

Early city clubs in North America followed a common pattern: started by a few (men) with a common interest in current events, politics, socializing, and coffee; started in a public space and eventually moved into their own space; expanded, consolidated and even merged with like clubs; and grappled with the changes in society. They continue to write their own history.

Exhibit 1.4: University Club of St. Louis

St. Louis (Missouri) was established in 1764, when fur trading was a dominant industry, largely controlled by French ex-patriots. The city was governed, at various times, by France and Spain, before becoming part of the USA in 1803. St. Louis became, and remained, an important gateway city in the late 1800s and early 1900s for migrants moving from east to west. The University Club of St. Louis was established during one of the city's growth periods, in 1872. It was started by a group of graduates and quickly grew to 120 members. Most university clubs had (and still have) an entry requirement which specifies a minimum of a college or university degree. The original bylaws of the University Club stated that 20% of members could be non-college graduates. The club was originally organized at a law office, held its first meeting in a courthouse and, eventually, leased private space of its own. As was often the case in the early days of clubs, several members broke off in 1878 to form the St. Louis Club. It moved three more times over a period of 20 years and built its own building in 1918. As additional university clubs formed, and as reciprocal agreements became more common, in 1912 it linked with other university clubs (Cleveland and Kansas City). An interesting chapter in the club's history involves how they survived Prohibition (due to a little creativity). The Club moved again in 1975 but encountered numerous challenges (not the least of which was a declining membership and a change in tax laws). The club closed in 2007.

Country clubs

Country clubs (usually focusing on golf) also have a long and rich history. It is understood that golf originated in Scotland but quickly spread to other continents (cricket, believed to have started in England, followed a similar pattern). Several of the early country clubs are profiled here.

The Royal and Ancient Golf Club of St Andrews

It is impossible to talk about clubs without talking about golf (most country clubs offer golf) and it is impossible to talk about golf without acknowledging The Royal and Ancient Golf Club of St Andrews (The R and A). The R and A is important for any number of reasons. First, it is generally regarded as being the first golf club, having been founded in 1754. However, whenever the question of which was the 'first club' arises, ambiguity occurs. For instance, in Scotland, the first club for which records still exist is the Company of Edinburgh Golfers. This club was founded in 1744 in Leith (10 years prior to the R and A), moved once, and then twice and is now known as the Honourable Company of Edinburgh Golfers and is located in Muirfield. The R and A was founded 10 years later but never changed locations, which is one of the reasons is has the current distinction. To complicate matters, records suggest that golf was being played in Scotland (in the Edinburgh area) since the 1550s and that various 'societies' existed in this part of Scotland dating back to the 1600s, the Society of Archers being one of the earliest. It is also reported that there were no fewer than six golfing 'societies' in and around the Edinburgh area in the 1700s. The societies eventually became more formalized, developed charters and established clubs and clubhouses. So, given the various accounts, The R and A is generally accepted as being the oldest.

The R and A celebrated its 250th anniversary in 2004, so now is over 260 years old. While the club was established in 1754, its current clubhouse was not built until 1854 (still over 160 years old!). It received its 'Royal' designation in 1834 by William IV (there are only 66 clubs in the world with the royal designation). The R and A has had a long and rich tradition. Archives from the club include early minutes of meetings and activities:

> "The minutes also give an insight into early club life. Members were to meet "once every fortnight by eleven of the clock ... and to play a round on the links. To dine together at Bailie Glass' and to pay each a shilling for his dinner, the absent as well as the present..." Bailie Glass' was a tavern in St Andrews. Before societies had their own clubhouses, it was customary for them to use local establishments as their meeting places, telling us much about the social nature of golf." (www.randa.org)

The formation of the early societies (which evolved into clubs such as The R and A and Muirfield) was the result of peoples' common interest in specific activities, desire to congregate, and desire to compete. As Behrend and Lewis point out:

> "Man is also companionable and gregarious and the social attitudes in the late seventeenth and eighteenth centuries had created an environment where people were beginning to form societies for a variety of reasons – political, philosophical, literary, historical, artistic. So, a group of like-minded people would meet regularly to indulge in their common interest, combining with it the pleasures of dining and drinking together ." (Behrend & Lewis, 1998, p.1).

Today, The R and A is comprised of a membership and a clubhouse. While the club is strongly associated with golf (and the game of golf), it does not own any courses. There are four courses in St Andrews but they are available for public use, although The R and A does receive tee times. Among other distinctions, The

R and A hosts the British Open golf tournament, and oversees administration and responsibility for the rules of golf.

Country clubs in India

As so often happens with fads, sports and almost everything else, ideas and activities get exported. Golf (and cricket) were introduced to India by the British resulting in the establishment of some early, well established, and long-lived clubs. One of the earliest is the Royal Calcutta Golf Club (1829). The club is said to be to India what St Andrews is to Scotland. It is renowned for, among other things, allowing women to use the facilities (as early as 1886), hosting prestigious golf tournaments, producing many excellent golfers, and its challenging course with its many natural water hazards. Like many clubs that started strictly as a golf club, it has evolved, now offering fitness, swimming, tennis and lawn bowling. Another early country club in India was the Royal Bombay Golf Club (established in 1842), now closed.

Country clubs in North America

Country clubs came later to North America although they too have a rich history. Five clubs are identified here as early forerunners; Philadelphia Cricket Club (1854); the Royal Montreal Golf Club (the oldest golf club in North America, established in 1873); Myopia Hunt Club (1875); Rockaway Hunting Club (1878); and The Country Club (1882). Of course, many clubs have come and gone since the 1700s and 1800s, records have been lost and clubs have closed and then reopened (and re-chartered) under the same names years apart (including the South Carolina Golf Club and the Savannah Golf Club). All of this can make it confusing for managers, historians and students alike. However, some clubs are deserving of our attention and have substantial historical documentation.

The Philadelphia Cricket Club was established in 1854, however it started as a cricket club and did not introduce golf until 1895. Still it qualifies as a country club, using our definition, and deserves recognition as one of the early clubs, regardless of activities offered. Today, it offers a variety of activities, including golf and cricket.

The Royal Montreal Golf Club (founded in 1873) is generally considered to be the oldest (continuously operating) golf club in North America, even preceding The Country Club and the Myopia Hunt Club. Golf came to Canada, as it did to the USA, via Scotland, and in the case of Canada, Scottish immigrants. It is believed that golf was introduced to Canada in 1824. The Royal Montreal Golf Club (RMGC) was instrumental in establishing golf as an important and respected activity in the country. Among other things, it helped establish the Royal Canadian Golf Association which included the RMGC, the Royal Quebec Golf Club, the Toronto Gulf Club and Royal Ottawa Golf Club. After several moves, the club moved to its current location on Ile Bizard in 1957. It currently offers 3 golf courses, 15 overnight guest rooms and other activities.

Photo 1.3: Colombia Country Club, Courtesy of the Library of Congress

Finally, Myopia Hunt Club also has a long and interesting history. It originated in 1875 (or 1876) in Winchester, Massachusetts, home to the Prince family. The Prince brothers (and friends) were a very active group and participated in a variety of sports including boating, tennis, baseball and hunting. The brothers, some friends, and friends of their friends, eventually established a club and clubhouse (in 1879) in Winchester. Because of the near-sightedness of the brothers, the club became known first as the Myopia Club and eventually, the Myopia Hunt Club. The club grew, evolved, and ended up in Hamilton where it is still today. Golf was introduced in 1894.

This is but a brief history of some of the early clubs. Other early (and current) clubs focused on other activities including yachting (Royal Cork Yacht Club); racquet sports (All England Lawn Tennis and Croquet Club; and the Calcutta Racquet Club); and even Tea Clubs (Thakubari Club). It is not possible (in the given space) to do justice to all of the early clubs whether they have come and gone or continue to operate. Nonetheless, students should now begin to appreciate the rich history of clubs. A more complete listing is included in Exhibit 1.5.

Exhibit 1.5: Important Dates in the History of Private Clubs

While the following dates are reliable and are supported by documentation, keep in mind that it can be difficult, if not impossible, to make definitive claims about the early cubs. This is because some of the very early clubs are long defunct, many clubs ceased operations for long periods of time, and many early records have been lost.

1693 – Opening of White's, considered to be the oldest continuously operating club in the British Commonwealth. Started as a group of 'gentlemen' meeting at White's Chocolate House in London and still operating. Boodle's and Brooks are other early London city clubs still in operation.

1720 – Records indicate that this is when the Royal Cork Yacht Club (Ireland) was formed making it the oldest yacht club in the world. Still operating.

1730s – Early US clubs including the South River Club (1732), established as a social club and the Schuylkill Fishing Company of Pennsylvania (1732) established as a fishing club.

1754 – Founding of the Royal and Ancient Golf Club (St Andrews), Scotland. Possible birthplace of golf, although open to dispute as the Company of Edinburgh Golfers was founded in 1744 (now Muirfield).

1762 – Boodle's (see above). Private city club in London. Still operating.

1764 – Brook's (see above). Private city club in London. Still operating.

1769 – Old Colony Club, Plymouth MA. Considered the oldest social club in the US. Had a hiatus in the 1800s and was reformed in 1875. Mostly a social club with activities revolving around food and beverage, special events and certain traditions. Still in operation.

1785 – The Beaver Club, Montreal. Members were associated with the North West Company (Montreal). Dissolved in 1824.

1786 – South Carolina Golf Club (in Charleston) was founded when this part of South Carolina was a hotbed of golf activity. Believed to have disbanded in 1800.

1793 – Calcutta Racquet Club – believed to be the oldest continuously operating racquet club in the world.

1794 – Savannah Golf Club – oldest golf club in the U.S (still in operation). Took a hiatus in the 1800s and reformed in 1899.

1827–1833 – very early clubs in India including the Bengal Club (1827), the Madras Club (1831) and the Byculla Club (1833).

1829 – Royal Calcutta Golf Club. Oldest, continuously operating golf club in India.

1834 – Philadelphia Club. Oldest city club in the US. Began with members meeting at Rubicam's Coffee House. In current location since 1850. Still in operation.

1836 – Union Club (NY). One of the very early city clubs in the US. Had antecedents dating to 1822. Moved to current location in 1933. Still in operation.

1837 – Toronto Club, Toronto. Shortly after the opening of the Philadelphia Club, the Toronto Club becomes the first city club in Canada. Still in operation.

1837 – Royal Nova Scotia Yacht Squadron (originally, the Royal Halifax Yacht Club).

1838 – The Australian Club (Sydney) and the Melbourne Club.

1844 – New York Yacht Club was founded. NYYC was the first yacht club in the US. Still in operation with clubhouses in NYC and Newport, Rhode Island.

1854 – Philadelphia Cricket Club – oldest country club in the US in continuous operation. Began as a cricket club and introduced golf in 1895. Still in operation.

1857 – St. James Club (Montreal). Opened in 1857 in rented space. Several members had been former members of an earlier club, the Beaver Club (for fur traders), dating to at least 1814. Moved to its current location in 1962. Still in operation.

1861 – The Dearborn Club. Early Midwestern club. Closed shortly after opening. Many members later started the Chicago Club.

1862 – Union League of Philadelphia (1862).

1865 – University Club of New York.

1868 – All England Lawn Tennis and Croquet Club (host of Wimbledon).

1869 – The Standard Club. An early Jewish membership club in Chicago. Preceded by three other Jewish clubs (all closed): Harmonie, Phoenix and Concordia Club.

1873 – Founding of the Royal Montreal Golf Club, which is the oldest golf club in Canada and North America. Given the 'Royal' designation in 1884 by Queen Victoria. Other golf clubs opened in Canada following the opening of the RMGC, including the Royal Quebec Golf Club (1874). Still in operation.

1875 – Founding of Myopia Hunt Club. Formed as the Myopia Club in 1875 and reformed as the Myopia Hunt Club in 1883. Has perhaps one of the most colorful histories, having been started by four brothers with a love for baseball, boating and tennis. Still in operation although golf, not hunting, is the main focus now.

1876 – Women's Club of Wisconsin. Seemingly, one of the earliest women's clubs. (Note: sometimes the records make it difficult to discern between private clubs for women and womens service clubs aiming to advance women's rights.

1876 – New Orleans Lawn Tennis Club. Believed to be the oldest lawn tennis club in the country.

1878 – Rockaway Hunting Club. Started as a hunting, polo and horse racing club. Continued to operate today primarily as a golf club but with other activities including tennis and squash.

1882 – Founding of The Country Club in Brookline, MA. Started as an equestrian and social club. Golf was introduced to members later (in 1893). Still in operation.

1884 – The Edgewood Club of Tivoli (NY). Started as a Tennis and polo club. Introduced golf later. Still in operation.

1887 – Club of Odd Volumes, a club devoted to literature, bookbinding and printing.

1889 – Founding of the Acorn Club in Philadelphia, an all womens club.

Why are clubs different?

The remainder of this book will focus primarily on two areas: (1) the various factors which make clubs different and (2) how these factors influence various management functions (such as governance, human resources, finance, etc.). First, though, we will briefly discuss two important aspects of the law and clubs, which apply in many different countries. Together, these help define what clubs are and how they operate.

Selection of members

Historically, clubs have been formed around discriminating who can be a member and who cannot. This is not unlike how we manage our individual lives – we choose (based on a variety of criteria) who can be our friends and who cannot. One manager we know, likens clubs to the treehouses that children often build, and choose who they allow to come up the tree. Clubs have historically discriminated on the basis of many factors including net worth, university attended, gender, race, profession, religion, etc. We will discuss this, first, in practical terms and then, in legal terms.

Clubs were started by people who wanted to be with others like themselves. Aristocrats wanted to be with aristocrats, politicians wanted to be with politicians, tea plantation owners wanted to be with other owners, ivy league graduates wanted to be with their own, petroleum engineers wanted to be with theirs, men wanted to be with other men, and so on. Early in their history, clubs were able to (and did) practice outright discrimination against what are now referred to as 'protected classes'. In the USA, women, African-Americans and Jews often found themselves on the outside looking in. As a result, these groups often started their own clubs, which themselves discriminated against the discriminators. Thus we had the Appomattox Club (a private club for African Americans, in Chicago), the Chilton Club (a private womens' club in Boston) and the Hillcrest Country Club (a private Jewish club in Los Angeles). Keep in mind, as we continue this discussion, that most of these, along with others which were predominately white, male and Protestant, have relaxed their policies as times have changed.

In the beginning, clubs discriminated because they wanted to and because they were allowed to by law. Fewer and fewer choose to do so now but the law (at least in the USA) protects their right to do so. Those clubs that are classified as non-profit (501 (c) 7's) are protected by the First Amendment of the Constitution and can retain their tax exempt status as long as they do not state in their bylaws (or elsewhere) that they discriminate (although some individual states have stricter laws). In the UK, the Equality Act (enacted in 2010) prohibits private clubs from discriminating.

So, depending on the country, clubs may continue to be allowed to discriminate, entitling them to maintain a 'homogeneous' membership base. Keep in mind that even in those countries that prohibit discrimination based upon race, creed, religion, gender, etc. a person may still not be accepted into the club of their choice because of their profession, age, or lack of a university degree.

Tax status

The other significant factor that impacts much of a club operation is their tax status. For instance, in the USA, if they are operating on a not-for-profit basis, they may be exempt from paying federal income taxes, within certain guidelines and with certain restrictions. This means that a club that is organized for social (or other reasons) may have revenues in excess of $10 million USD but will not have to pay taxes on this. They will have to pay other taxes which would include payroll taxes, sales taxes, and property taxes, among others. In the UK, they are exempt from paying VAT taxes.

As you will imagine, having tax exemptions means that money can be used for other things but at the same time, comes with certain responsibilities. These will be discussed further in the chapter on club finances.

Changes in clubs

One of the themes in this book will be the many changes that clubs have gone through in the last ten to twenty years. As society has changed, so have clubs specifically with respect to their operations (greater use of technology); their membership (more women and families); economics (many clubs have struggled financially); activities (the decreasing interest in golf and increased interest in fitness); legal (changes in tax laws); and the fact that clubs are simply becoming more 'full-service' destinations. These and other topics will be explored more fully in every chapter and, especially, in Chapter 10.

Summary

In this chapter, we have introduced students to the world of private clubs (ClubWorld) discussing some of the things that make them different, why they exist, some of their primary activities, their history, a little bit about their size and scope, and two of the factors that allow them to be treated differently (admissions policies and tax exemptions). The next chapter looks more fully at the different types of clubs and their operations.

Discussion questions

1   Identify one of the early clubs in your region. How much documented history is there? Is it still in existence? How would you classify it? How did it change over time?

2   Identify one or two of the things that distinguish private clubs from public accommodations (hotels and restaurants). Discuss how you think these distinguishing factors would affect the management of operations.

3   What are some examples of laws that affect clubs in your region/country? How are they viewed by the government?

References

Bourke, A. (1892). *The History of White's*. Bourke: London.

Chaster, A. W. (1903). *Wertheimer's Law Relating to Clubs*. Stevens and Haynes: Temple Bar.

The Royal and Ancient. www.randa.org

Wister, O. (1934) *The Philadelphia Club: 1834 – 1934*. The Philadelphia Club: Philadelphia.

2 The Evolution of a Club

"I BELIEVE IT'S TIME TO FORM A CLUB."

The CHARTER

This society shall be organized and registered under this Act and heretofore will be known as "The Club" on this first day of June, 1875. The 20 founding members agree to add new members to a maximum of 50 for an admission price of $20

"I'VE JUST RETURNED FROM SCOTLAND AND LEARNED ABOUT THIS GAME THEY CALL 'GOLF.'"

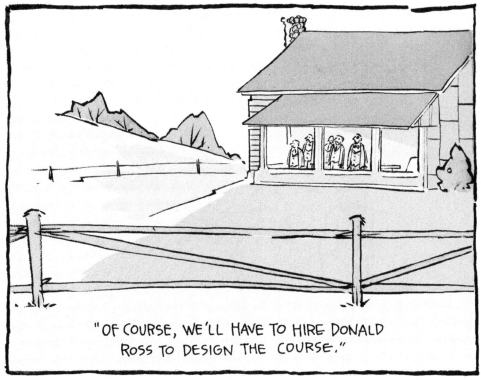

"OF COURSE, WE'LL HAVE TO HIRE DONALD ROSS TO DESIGN THE COURSE."

D. ROSS - b. 1872, SCOTLAND.
MOVED to U.S. in 1899, WHERE
HE DESIGNED OVER 400 GOLF
COURSES, ESTABLISHING HIMSELF
as the PREEMINENT GOLF COURSE
ARCHITECT of HIS TIME.

" THE WOMEN ARE SHOWING MORE INTEREST IN THE CLUB, SHOULD WE ALLOW THEM TO ATTEND SOME EVENTS?"

" ITS TIME WE TALKED ABOUT ALLOWING WOMEN TO BE EQUAL MEMBERS AND BE ALLOWED ON THE BOARD."

3 Types of Clubs

Introduction

Clubs come in so many different types and forms, that it becomes necessary to classify them, much the way we do with hotels. Hotels may be classified by size (number of guest rooms), service level (economy to luxury), price (based on average rate), location, etc. Clubs are classified in a slightly different way. When we discuss the types of clubs that exist, we can do so in six different ways:

1 By primary activity/location

2 By clientele

3 Equity/nonequity

4 Size (by number of members, gross volume, or initiation fee)

5 By ownership

6 Tax status

It is important to understand how and why we classify clubs in these ways, and who does so. In short, though, we classify them for the same reasons that we might classify hotels, restaurants, or other types of businesses – to be able to group similar clubs with one another and for comparison purposes. For instance, it would be unreasonable, and counterproductive, to group 'city clubs' and 'country clubs' together because of their different purposes and mixes of services. Yes, they all have private membership and high levels of service and traditions but they are very different in other regards (including location and services). So, instead, it makes more sense to discuss them in the context of similar operations, just as we would refrain from discussing quick-service restaurants and fine dining restaurants together. While they might have some similarity (they both serve food), one could just as easily argue that they represent different corners of the same industry.

Classifying clubs by primary activity/location

Primary activity is perhaps the most common way to classify clubs and, in fact, this is the way that much of the industry and companies that serve the industry use. By primary activity, we are referring to the singular activity that motivates members to become a member of a club. For instance, the most common example would be a golf club. Or a yacht club. Or a tennis club. Or a hunt club. It gets a little confusing when we couple **primary activity** with **location**. We do this for a good reason though – they often mean (or, at least, suggest) the same thing. We commonly refer to 'country clubs' or 'city clubs'. When we do so, we are obviously referring to location, but it also infers activity. For instance, country clubs (usually) offer golf. And city clubs often offer a mix of dining, athletics and rooms. Yacht clubs, also, denote an activity but also indicate where they are located (on the water). So, it is important to remember that there is a correlation between location and activity, although not a perfect one. But back to classifying clubs by activity. Primary activities may involve (but are not limited to):

- Golf/Country
- Dining/City/University
- Yachting
- Racquet (tennis, squash, badminton, paddle tennis, pickleball)
- Aquatics
- Cricket
- Hunting
- Fitness/athletics
- Arts (and letters)
- Equestrian/polo
- Aeronautics
- Auto/motorcycle (common in Europe)
- Curling
- Alpine ski/snowboarding (common in Canada)
- Military clubs

No list could possibly be comprehensive since it would have to include almost every activity that people engage in at clubs. Not all of these will be discussed in detail but some of the (more) common types of clubs, and associated activities, are discussed below.

Golf/country clubs

Golf clubs are clubs whose primary (and sometimes, only) activity is golf. Occasionally, the term golf club and country club will be used synonymously. Golf is a popular activity, although declining in popularity. Since country clubs outnumber golf clubs, let's discuss country clubs in little more detail.

Country clubs typically offer a variety of activities, in addition to golf, such as tennis, paddle tennis, fitness, aquatics, and even bowling. The number and range of activities is virtually unlimited, especially in those clubs that operate year round and may offer multiple seasonal activities. One of the authors worked at a private club in Connecticut which had 500 members, 18 holes of golf, several tennis and paddle tennis courts, a swimming pool, three dining rooms and a ballroom for banquets. This is not an uncommon mix of activities and facilities for a club of this size. Such a club would also need to hire skilled professionals in each of these areas. Country clubs have begun to offer additional activities and services to their members, such as fitness. This will be discussed in more detail in later chapters.

Photo 3.1: Manchester Country Club, by Gil Talbot Photography, courtesy of Manchester Country Club.

Continuing with this example, a club of this size would have multiple membership categories, of which the one with the most members would usually be the 'full' member category, which would allow those members to golf. The club would also have multiple other membership categories (discussed more in Chapter 8). However, golf would most likely dominate the club, the general manager would have to have a good understanding of the game, and the primary season would begin and end with that of the golf season.

Keep in mind that seasonality is a major factor in clubs, particularly those involving outdoor activities (this is true regardless of hemisphere). Seasonality affects operations, activities and the budget. In some climates, it is too hot to play golf (or other sports) in some seasons and too cold in others. As a result, some clubs close, or scale down operations, for a portion of the year, from a few weeks to a few months. That said, one of the trends in country clubs is to offer activities for 12 months out of the year by introducing new activities that are not season specific. Seasonality is not limited to country clubs, however.

One of the best examples of a club that we have seen, which did a great job of leveraging seasonal activities, was a country club in Canada. It offered both golf and curling, which is a winter sport played on ice. Because of the ways that the respective seasons of these two sports ran, they were able to begin one activity, just as the other was finishing its season. This also allowed the club to create separate membership categories and to maximize year-round usage of the club.

Dining/city clubs

Another major category of clubs are dining clubs. Again, we will discuss these in the context of the larger category, city clubs. One of the primary activities is dining which may take place in one or more dining rooms. Many of the older city clubs (for instance in Sydney, Philadelphia, Belfast, Mumbai, or London), are located in historic buildings with many rooms which have been converted for dining.

In many instances, city clubs also double as 'hotels' for their members (and guests). This is an added feature that can be used by members who have to stay overnight in the city, often times for business. Rooms are also often occupied by guests who are members of 'reciprocal clubs', clubs which have a formal agreement with one another – extending privileges to each other's members. Clubs may have just a few rooms to many. Two examples are the New York Athletic Club which offers 187 guest rooms and the Union League Club (of Chicago) which has 180 rooms. Both of these are veritable hotels, although they offer much more to their members.

Many city clubs also offer athletics (such as the clubs mentioned above). Squash and racquetball are common activities at city clubs as are swimming and fitness. Others may offer bowling, boxing, basketball, badminton, skating and/or fencing. While others have begun offering classes in martial arts, Pilates, Barre and Zumba.

What a club chooses to offer is often based on traditions, current trends, member demands and what the physical facility will allow. One club in downtown Toronto offers over 12 different athletic activities to members. Sometimes, if their focus is exclusively on athletics, clubs will be known as athletic clubs but these should not be confused with for-profit chains like Planet Fitness, Gold's Gym, GymBox, Fitness First and Equinox.

Photo 3.2: Karachi Club – Swimming Pool

That said, some well-established city clubs do not offer any athletics at all. For instance, the Union Club (Boston), which was established in 1863, focuses on dining and member events. They also have 14 overnight guest rooms. So, its members do not join the Union Club for athletics but more for social activities and comradery.

Exhibit 3.1: Ulster Reform Club

The Ulster Reform Club, located in Belfast, Northern Ireland, is a unique club in many respects. A classic city club (because of its location and its offerings), the club is the result of a joiner first with the Union Club (established in 1837) in 1953, and later merging with the Ulster Club (established in 1857) in 1982. The club occupies a majestic and historic building in the centre of Belfast and is the last remaining city club in the area. The five story building houses a grand dining room, a bar, a reading room, a fitness facility, a snooker room and multiple smaller meeting rooms. It has no overnight guest rooms at this time.

It is an active club – a glance at a recent club calendar indicates that upcoming events include shooting competitions, golf tournaments, an Italian themed wine and food event, and a speaker series. They have reciprocal agreements with clubs around the world. It is a traditional club in that they have retained many traditional customs regarding dress and etiquette. For instance, the club is restricted to members, their guests and reciprocal members; proper dress is required; and mobile telephones are restricted. The club is governed by the laws under the Registration of Clubs (Northern Ireland) order which defines how the club is structured and governed. For instance, one of the regulations states that; "The business and affairs of the club shall be under the management of a committee or governing body consisting of a secretary, a treasurer and not less than 5 ordinary or life members who are elected to the committee or body for not less than 1 year by the general body of members having rights of voting in relation to the affairs of the club."

The history of the club has been documented with the publication of *The Ulster Reform Club, Past and Present*.

University clubs

A close relation to the city club, is the university club whose main difference is in its membership policies. These exist all over the world, are typically located in city centres, and historically have only accepted members with college or university degrees, although some have relaxed these requirements in recent years. For instance, the Harvard Club (in Boston) has recently opened membership in their Back Bay location to graduates of MIT, Yale and the Fletcher School of Diplomacy (at Tufts). They also open membership to their downtown location to graduates of other colleges and universities, not limited to those above.

Some university clubs are strictly for graduates of a specific university (Yale, Harvard, Oxford and Cambridge), while others are open to graduates from different universities. Their names tend to be descriptive of where they are and who they are – the University Club of New York, University Club of Boston, etc. Among those which are called university clubs, the University Club of New York, founded in 1865, is the oldest in the USA.

According to Neal Vohr, CCM, CCE, general manager of the University Club of Boston, university clubs were based on the premise of "celebrating individual academic achievement." While clubs which have the word 'university' in their name have that in common, and common admissions policies, they have other characteristics in common as well. They tend to focus on athletics, often squash, and have multiple sport programs. Many of them also have overnight accommodations, as do other types of city clubs.

University clubs typically operate as separate entities from the universities with which they are associated, if they are affiliated with a particular university. Their services and activities are similar to regular city clubs, with dining, special events, rooms and athletics. More and more university clubs (and city clubs in general) are offering cooking classes, literary events, and even boxing matches! These are all being offered to engage members, attract new members and give value to memberships.

Yacht clubs

Yacht clubs are an entirely different type of club, altogether. They bring together members who are interested in boating (usually defined as sailing but interest in power boats is increasing). They also offer some of the other amenities already mentioned.

Some of the oldest yacht clubs in North America include the Southern Yacht Club (in New Orleans), the New York Yacht Club (in New York and Newport) and the Royal Nova Scotia Yacht Squadron (in Halifax). Yacht clubs exist throughout the world though including India (Royal Connaught Boat Club), Hong Kong (Royal Hong Kong Yacht Club), Ireland (Royal Cork Yacht Club), Bermuda (Royal Bermuda Yacht Club), and Australia (Royal Sydney Yacht Squadron).

Yacht clubs are different in many ways. Instead of just being stewards of buildings and land, they are stewards of the water, which carries many responsibilities (not the least of which is water safety). Since they own land along the coast (and water rights) they are governed by applicable laws and must be accountable to such agencies as the Maritime and Coast Guard Agency, environmental agencies and others. They need to be aware of regulations concerning clean water, storm water, dockings and moorings, navigable water guidelines, etc.

Aside from the environmental and legal considerations, they are different in other ways, three which we would like to identify here. First, while their general organizations structure may be the same as other clubs, the titles of officer positions and their responsibilities are different. The executive committee positions include commodore, vice-commodore and rear commodore (along with the usual positions of secretary and treasurer). There may also be additional positions, such as Measurer, which do not exist in other types of clubs.

Second, clubs thrive on membership activities and yacht clubs are no different in this respect. However, the major member activity in yacht clubs is likely to be a 'regatta' or race. Regattas tend to be major events, often involving other clubs, and consist of the race itself, but also food and beverage, awards, etc. They also require extensive planning. One of the most famous regattas in the world is the America's Cup, which started in 1851 and is a competition amongst yacht clubs around the world. The Royal New Zealand Yacht Squadron is the current cup holder.

Finally, the third differentiator is the role that *reciprocal agreements* play in yacht clubs. Reciprocal agreements are where members of one club can use the services of another. Yacht clubs have taken this concept to a near art form for one very good reason – members of one club like to sail to different clubs and be allowed docking rights, mooring privileges, or even a room in the clubhouse. Stories are told about members who essentially 'club hop' their way around the world. To give one example of how extensive these agreements might be, the Royal New Zealand Yacht Squadron lists some 50 reciprocal clubs on their web site.

So, yacht clubs attract members who have an interest in boating, and, collectively, try to increase the interest in boating (and other water sports). It would not be unusual for a member of a yacht club to also belong to another type of club, to mollify their other interests.

Racquet clubs

Another type of club that exists are racquet clubs. Racquet sports in general are popular in clubs but tennis and squash continue to prevail. We will consider one specific type of racquet club here - tennis clubs. A profile of the New Orleans Lawn Tennis Club is discussed in Exhibit 3.2.

Tennis clubs also have a long and illustrious history as tennis is an old game. Tennis, as we know it, was probably established in the late 1800s in England and quickly transported around the world. Tennis clubs typically offer tennis (of course) but may also offer other racquet sports, aquatics, fitness and food and beverage. Some of the activities that tennis (or other racquet clubs) offer their members include extensive intra-club activities, competitions/ tournaments and 'ladders'. Because of the number of matches and the level of competition, it is also very common to have designated spectator areas. Tennis (or racquet) clubs also offer extensive children's programs, lessons/coaching and, often, more than one other racquet sport. In addition, with the advent of all-weather surfaces and covered courts, tennis has become a year round sport, allowing such clubs to remain active for 12 months.

Exhibit 3.2: New Orleans Lawn Tennis Club

It is sad to think of the number of written records, photos, documentation and artifacts from the early days of clubs, which have been lost. Not so with the New Orleans Lawn Tennis Club, established in 1876. As he recounts in his book *The New Orleans Lawn Tennis Club: The Oldest in the Americas*, Richard Wolfe describes the hand-written minutes from the first meeting in 1876, which still survive. He goes on to explain how and why a tennis club of this stature, and located where it was, should have been the first in the USA, rather than one in Boston, Philadelphia or New York. The answer is explained by the specific time and place that the cotton industry and British ex-pats came together. They had an interest in wanting to continue to play tennis and assured this happened with the founding of the NOLTC. Early records even show purchases of tennis balls, imported from England.

The NOLTC has since moved from its original location, although it is still in New Orleans. Its primary focus is still on tennis but also has a vibrant food and beverage programme as well as a pool and fitness centre.

Because of the long history of tennis, the number of clubs which offer it, and the sense of comradery, there is an association for tennis clubs that are at least 100 years old, called The Association of Centenary Tennis Clubs. It is an international association with member clubs in North America, South America, Europe, Asia and Australia. Its mission is to "uphold the traditions of tennis, as well as the spirit of fair play which is inherent to this great sport." Some of its members include the Buenos Aires Lawn Tennis Club (Argentina), the Kooyong Lawn Tennis Club (Australia), and the Delhi Gymkhana Club.

There are a myriad of other types of clubs, as defined by primary activity. Keep in mind though that clubs evolve over time and will be established on one type of activity, then convert as member interests change or as society changes. For instance, many clubs that started as hunt clubs have changed their mission as hunting has become more restricted and as cities have encroached on their once remote locations. Other examples would be cricket and polo clubs (two activities that were popular in the USA in the 1800s but less so now). Many of these clubs changed their focus with the advent of golf in the late 1800s. Often these clubs will maintain a connection to their past though by offering these older activities, albeit on a more limited basis.

Photo 3.3: Rock Creek Hunt Club, Library of Congress

Exhibit 3.3: Military clubs

Military clubs are a special type of club, restricted to a specific type of membership. The Army and Navy Club, located in Washington D.C., is one such historic club. As their website states:

"Since our formation as a Club in 1885, The Army and Navy Club has been a home away from home for our country's military officers. We are known for, and take pride in, our superior facilities, emphasis on fine food and wines, extraordinary Library, special events designed to benefit our members, the warmth and dedication of our staff, and the special camaraderie enjoyed by our members and guests… We endeavor to collect, restore, document and display military themed artworks and books to enrich the understanding of our role in our country's history. We do this through our very active Library Trust Fund, a tax exempt 501(c)(3) entity that raises the funds necessary to improve our book and fine art collection and sponsor related events. We also have an active research program piloted by the Club Historian… We offer 32 hotel rooms, an awe inspiring collection of original military art, a fabled military Library, Main Dining Room, Grill, Ballroom, Daiquiri Lounge, multiple meeting rooms, indoor racquetball and squash courts, weight room and quality locker rooms for both our male and female members." (https://www.armynavyclub.org/club/history)

The UK also has its share of military clubs. The Royal Air Force Club, which was founded in 1918, focuses not only on the Royal Air Force, but also on aviation throughout UK.

The club, located in the Piccadilly area of London, is open to "serving and former serving Officers of the RAF and Allied Air Forces." In addition to guest rooms, extensive food and beverage offerings, and a library, the clubs serve to document the history of aviation and the Royal Air Force.

No discussion of military clubs would be complete without mentioning the United Service Club, one of the earliest military clubs, which was founded in 1815 and catered to officers in the British Army and Royal Navy. The club suffered membership and financial challenges and closed in the 1970s.

Military clubs, just like clubs of other types, have been forced to change with the times. An article in the *San Diego Union-Tribune* discusses some of the changes that these clubs have made over the last decade, including changing membership requirements, expanding services, repurposing the spaces or even closing. One of the most significant changes that many military clubs has made is in expanding their membership beyond officers, to included enlisted personnel. "...the closures are fostering a new social order in the military, one where comradeship and cohesion are based more on a top-to-bottom unit allegiance rather than the stratified worlds of officers and the enlisted. At Camp Pendleton, one of the officers' clubs was converted last year into a family-readiness center. A portion of the old club was renovated and reopened a few months ago as Pub 1795, named after its building number. From 4 to 9 p.m. Fridays, it's open for officers only. The rest of the time, the Marines use it for classes, meetings and events such as retirement parties." http://www.sandiegouniontribune.com/sdut-military-combination-of-enlisted-and-officers-2010feb22-story.html.

Classifying clubs by membership

Clubs may also be classified by the type of member that they attract (or even restrict their membership to). This simply means that the club focuses on a particular type of member, however defined. Some clubs might focus on members within a certain profession, such as petroleum engineers. The former Petroleum Club in New Orleans would be an example of this. The Ranchmen's Club (cattlemen) and the Beaver Club (fur trade), both profiled in Chapter 1, would be examples of attracting members associated with a certain trade or industry. There are also clubs for artists, university faculty, military personnel, and a variety of other professions. There are even clubs for members in the book and publishing businesses. One such club is the Club of Odd Volumes, whose bylaws state: "This Club is formed for the purpose of promoting literary and artistic tastes, establishing and maintaining a place for social meetings and a reference library, providing occasional exhibits of a special and instructive character, and publishing rare prints and books relating to historical and literary matters." The candidates for membership were required to be "men sincerely interested in the objects named."

In addition to limiting membership by profession, clubs might also attract members defined by their station in life, such as where they are from or where they went to school. We have already talked about clubs for graduates of a certain university but there are clubs dedicated to members who are living abroad (such as Americans living in Japan or UK residents living in India). We would also include military clubs here – those that are either for current military personnel or retired (for example, the Army and Navy Club or the Royal Air Force Club, in London).

Clubs at one time were established around political affiliations or beliefs, such as the various Union clubs in the USA, for instance, the Union League in Philadelphia (Exhibit 3.4). This is becoming less common but many clubs are still dominated by members of a certain political parties.

Exhibit 3.4: The Union League Club

The 1860s in the USA brought tremendous change and divisions within society. The Union League Club (originally, the Union Club), established in 1862, was at the heart of it. The club was started by a group of prominent Philadelphians who supported Abraham Lincoln, anti-slavery and pro-union. It was suggested that forming a club, with a clubhouse for meetings, would contribute to their cause. George Boker and John Hare, both community stalwarts, were the forces behind the club. Mutual feelings around anti-slavery, pro-Unionism and civic engagement led to the founding of the club for like-minded members.

There were only three articles in the original bylaws (in addition to the name of the newly formed club): Article II required that members show "unqualified loyalty to the government" and capped membership at 50; Article III specified where and when members would meet and that the wines should be "limited to Sherry and Madeira" and; Article IV put limits on guests of members.

Some of their early initiatives included raising money for the protection of the city from an attack by the Confederacy. They also contributed resources and effort to the reëlection of President Lincoln.

The Union League Club continues to be a prominent club today. "Today, the Union League is home to over 3,500 men and women who contribute to club life and keep alive the League's traditions. As they did in 1862, today's members represent the Philadelphia region's leaders in business, education, technology, healthcare, law,

> government, religion, art and culture. The League's civic participation and philanthropic outreach takes the form of three charitable foundations: The Youth Work Foundation, The Scholarship Foundation and The Abraham Lincoln Foundation, which educate the public about our nation's history, recognize student role models in our region's schools, and provide scholarships to deserving students. "(https://www.unionleague.org/about.php)

Back in the last century, when clubs were more outwardly discriminatory, they also formed around gender, race, and religion affiliations. At a time when the doors of more traditional clubs were closed to African-Americans, women and Jews (among others), these same groups started their own clubs to serve their communities. Tumblebrook Country Club (in Bloomfield, Connecticut) is one example and is profiled in Exhibit 3.5.

Exhibit 3.5: Tumble Brook Country Club

Tumble Brook Country Club (in Bloomfield, Connecticut) was founded in 1922, during a time when Jews faced a great deal of discrimination. Tumble Brook, whose primary activity was golf, grew out of the Touro Club, a Jewish social club which originally limited its membership to Jews of German descent. According to Becker and Pearson, "By 1910, East European Jews in Hartford outnumbered German Jews by five to one. As in other cities where the pattern held, German Jews resented the newcomers and looked down upon them. They tried to keep the new arrivals out of their synagogues, clubs, schools and, above all, from marrying their sons and daughters. For example, membership in the Touro Club, founded in 1901, was restricted initially to Jews of German background."

Jewish clubs in general, and Tumble Brook in particular supported (and in some cases continue to support) the Jewish community. In some Jewish clubs, the expectation would be for members to contribute to Jewish charitable organizations, such as United Jewish Appeal, the Jewish Federations of North America and others.

The club is based on 136 acres in the suburbs of Hartford on what used to be an old farm. It offers golf, tennis, swimming and paddle tennis, along with extensive food and beverage offerings. According to a former manager, it has recently begun to expand its membership beyond its original Jewish base of members. It has also recently contracted with a club management company, Troon.

Students may also sometimes hear a club referred to by its clientele. For instance a club may be referred to as a 'Jewish club' (suggesting that the primary makeup of members is Jewish), a 'Women's club' (where the members are predominantly women) or a 'Faculty club' which are typically located on university campuses and cater to faculty (and staff). This usually means that that was how the club was originally established and may or may not have any bearing on the current state of affairs. In fact, because of changes in society, many of these clubs have opened their doors to the broader community, and sometimes encountered challenges in doing so. In short, there is a club for every type of person regardless profession, affiliation or interests. That said, old barriers are being broken down and it is not as easy to classify clubs in such simple terms anymore.

Classifying clubs by size

It is also common (and helpful) to discuss clubs in the context of their size. Size is typically measured by number of members or annual revenues. Again, the purpose for classifying them in this way is to compare clubs with a similar number of members (or annual revenues) in terms of the number of activities, costs, member engagement, member turnover, etc. Clubs may range in size from under 100 members to 10,000 or more. The clubs with which we typically interact have an average of about 750 members.

In addition, clubs may range in annual revenues from well under $1 million USD to over $20 million USD. The annual revenues (or gross receipts) are primarily a function of the number of members, the amount of dues and the amount of Nonmember business.

As an example, PKF, a leading accounting and consulting company, publishes an annual report on club operations and financial performance. In it, they segment clubs into three categories: (1) under 500 members; (2) 500 – 700 members and; (3) over 700 members. Again, this helps clubs to compare themselves with others of similar size (they also discuss city clubs and country clubs separately).

Equity/nonequity

Clubs are often referred to as either 'equity' or 'nonequity' (or proprietary) clubs. These terms have a specific meaning but, at the same time, are rife with misunderstanding. We have even heard managers misuse the terms. It is important that students understand the meaning of their terms as well as all of their implications.

An equity club is one in which the member owns some form of equity. According to Mitchell Stump, of the Club Tax Network, an equity club is "generally a member-owned club where members have voting rights and liquidation rights." Think of it as owning stock in a business. This ownership gives the member/owner certain rights and privileges. In contrast, a nonequity club is one in which a member does not retain ownership nor do they usually have any associated rights and privileges aside from those that membership provides. These clubs are typically owned by companies, developers, and the like.

At this point, it is important to point out that equity is not synonymous with refundable, even though some people use these terms interchangeably. Refundable means that the equity payment (usually paid as the initiation fee) is refundable (fully or partially) when the member leaves the club. While it is true that most clubs that have refundable memberships are equity clubs and that most clubs that do not are nonequity clubs, this does not always hold true. Figure 3.1 shows indicates how these different types of clubs overlap.

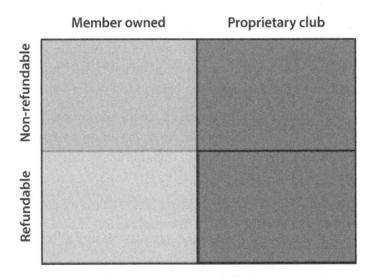

Figure 3.1: Club ownership models: Adapted from ClubBenchmarking

There have been tremendous changes in the overall mix of equity and nonequity clubs in recent years. As some equity clubs have struggled in recent years, several have either (1) been taken over by professional management companies (2) converted to semi-public facilities or (3) been purchased outright by private companies. Further, most of the newer clubs that have opened in recent years have been of the nonequity variety, suggesting a preference by younger members for these types of clubs and the viability of a different financial model.

Classifying clubs by ownership

When we refer to ownership, we are speaking of who actually owns the club. This is important because it has all sorts of implications including mission, governance, operations and tax status (financial). Most clubs are owned by either (1) the members of the club or; (2) an individual owner/company/developer, which may be known as a proprietary club. In the former instance, if a club is owned by its members, it is generally operated as tax-exempt, as a 501 (c) 7 in the USA. In the latter case, where it is owned by a person or entity, the club is generally operated on a for-profit basis. And of course, hybrid clubs exist as well. As one can imagine, the ownership model has far reaching implications.

Member-owned clubs

Member-owned clubs tend to operate in a specific way, being service driven, operating on a break-even basis, and having a certain governance model (largely driven by its members). Perhaps the greatest factor which differentiates them is the extent of member involvement in almost every aspect of the club. This would range from determining the scope, mission and strategic direction of the club, establishing (and changing) bylaws, decisions on new members, capital spending, new programmes, etc. Members would also appoint a general manager (through a board).

A member-owned (and equity) club would not be profit driven. Rather, it would operate on a break-even basis where the revenue would be used to finance the operating budget and the surplus would be reinvested in the club. As a result of this, pricing would be more conservative, and the culture would be more customer service driven rather than marketing driven. Also, dues would be used to subsidize many of the member programmes and activities. The average member owned club generates 50 percent of its revenue from dues while offering many services to its members for 'free'.

These types of clubs also tend to be different, structurally and operationally. Day to day activities would be overseen by a general manager while the board would look after the long term interests of the club. The interests of the club are also monitored by committees, which are generally composed of several members, chaired by a member of the board, and include a member of the management staff. There are committees for almost every major area of a club. In a country club, an important one would be the Greens Committee, which would be involved with advising the board about matters relating to the ongoing operation of the golf course. In a city club, the Program Committee would oversee the ongoing programming of events for its members. And in a yacht club, one of the most critical would be the Race and Regatta Committee which would oversee the policies around races and the management of them. These are just a few examples.

The general manager in a member owned club would have a series of direct reports, or department heads, with each department head overseeing a functional area such as golf, grounds, food and beverage, or tennis. The role of the general manager, board of directors and committees are discussed in more detail in Chapter 4.

Developer owned clubs

So far, we have discussed member owned clubs and proprietary clubs. However, there are two other classifications of clubs which exist and do not fit neatly into these categories. The first are those owned and operated by a 'developer'. Many of these, particularly in the southern USA include a housing development, typically of detached single-family homes, with some located in gated communities. Developers often view two things as contributing to increasing the value of home lots – if the lots are located on either the waterfront or on a golf course. As a result, many housing developments have been developed along with golf courses, and sometimes, full service country clubs. When developers include golf courses and/or clubs, several things may transpire once all of the houses and club memberships are sold. First, the developer may retain ownership and management of the club, especially if the developer has a golf or club management division within their company. Alternatively, it may be sold or contracted to a third part management company. Finally, it may be turned over to the Home Owners Association (HOA), or equivalent, to be run by the members.

Semi-private clubs

The final type of club which is a bit different, based on ownership, is referred to as semi-public, or semi-private. These clubs are a hybrid between member-owned and for-profit clubs, where there is a core group of members who have membership privileges but may not retain any ownership stake. Members retain preferred tee times and then the course is open to the public during other, less desirable, times. The dining room is also usually open to the public. This model has a couple of advantages. Essentially, it is run similarly to a private club but the nonmember revenues subsidize member activities.

According to Hal Phillips, Managing Director of Mandarin Media, a communications agency specializing in the golf, hospitality and property industries, the concept of semi-private clubs changed a few years ago. In the early 2000s, they were dominated by what were essentially daily fee golf courses which offered seasonal memberships, allowing individuals either unlimited play, or a specific number of rounds. According to Phillips, the concept began to change from public courses trying to appear to be private, to private courses offering a public component. This typically came about when a private club was struggling financially and needed a new revenue stream. So, some were able to maintain their not-for-profit status while offering certain tee times to the public, as long as the amount of revenue did not jeopardize their tax status. In the latter model, the club would be run as a member-owned club, described above, with a general manager and board structure.

Finally, there are a number of club management companies which own and/or manage clubs for a profit. In some cases, they manage for-profit clubs while in other cases, they may manage equity clubs for it members under a management fee.

Classifying clubs by tax status

Finally, clubs may be classified on the basis of their tax status. Simply, they either pay taxes or they do not. Many countries allow private, not-for-profit clubs, assuming they meet certain criteria, to be exempt from paying federal income tax. This means that the sales that they take in for joining fees, dues, greens fees, food and beverage, rooms, etc. are exempt from being taxed as revenue. Again, there are lots of rules and regulations around this, which are discussed in greater detail in Chapter 9. And it is important to remember that they are still obligated to pay property tax, payroll taxes, and sales tax (or VAT) so this exemption is usually limited to the payment of federal income tax.

In the United States, those clubs that are classified as 501(c)7s are able to maintain their tax status (and not pay federal income tax) but must adhere to certain restrictions and regulations. The two that we will concern ourselves with here are the 15%/35% Rule and the rule around advertising.

The IRS has stated that "Where a club makes its facilities available to the general public to a substantial degree, the club is not operated exclusively for pleasure, recreation, or other nonprofitable purposes. Specifically, social clubs can receive up to 35% of their gross receipts, including investment income, from sources outside their membership. Within the 35%, not more than 15% of gross receipts should be derived from the use of the social club's facilities or services by the general public (nonmembers). If a club exceeds the 35/15% test, facts and circumstances are applied to determine if substantially all of its activities are for pleasure, recreation and other nonprofitable purposes." Essentially what this means, is that clubs must carefully monitor the level of nonmember income being generated so as not to exceed the limit, thus jeopardizing their status.

In addition, 501(c)7s are restricted as to the amount of advertising they are allowed to do. According to the IRS: "A club which engages in business, such as making its social and recreational facilities available to the general public or by selling real estate, timber, or other products, is not organized and operated exclusively for pleasure, recreation, and other nonprofitable purposes, and is not exempt under section 501(a). Solicitation by advertisement or otherwise for public patronage of its facilities is prima facie evidence that the club is engaging in business and is not being operated exclusively for pleasure, recreation, or social purposes. However, an incidental sale of property will not deprive a club of its exemption."

Regarding sales tax, this is dependent upon the state, province or country where the club is located. However, in some cases, usage (such as food and beverage) is exempt from sales tax while membership fees (initiation and dues) are subject to sales tax. Thus, the club would charge members tax on these fees and the taxes would be passed along to the appropriate tax authority.

The way in which property taxes are levied are equally varied and will depend on how a local municipality assesses a club. That said, many nonprofit clubs are given a tax reduction, based upon valuation, their tax status, age, mission, land usage, or other reason. For instance, one state in the northeastern USA allows a 75 % property tax reduction to country clubs based upon recreational uses and preservation of open land. Valuation of property may be based on different things but two popular methods include the (1) income method and the (2) highest and best economic use. Again, there are many variables which determine how much property tax a club will pay, but more often than not, it is at a 'reduced' rate.

Summary

We have discussed a variety of types of clubs, their characteristics, and how they might be classified. It is important to remember though that there are always exceptions and examples of clubs that might not fit into any of our predetermined categories. The exciting thing about clubs is that no two are exactly alike but they do have characteristics in common which help us to classify them for comparison purposes.

The next few chapters will look more closely at how clubs are organized, governed and operated.

Discussion questions

1 Identify a club in your area that is unique and does not quite fit into the categories we have created. How would you describe and classify it?

2 Conduct an inventory of private clubs in your area. Classify them in the ways that were discussed in the chapter.

3 What is the tax classification for not-for-profit clubs in your area? What restrictions are they under in order to maintain their tax status?

References

Army and Navy Club, https://www.armynavyclub.org/club/history

Becker, H. & Pearson, R. (1979). The Jewish Community of Hartford, Connecticut, 1880-1929. www.AmericanJewishArchives.org

Chambers, G. & Roulston, W. (2009). The Ulster Reform Club, Past and Present. Ulster Reform Club and Ulster Historical Society: Belfast.

San Diego Union-Tribune, http://www.sandiegouniontribune.com/sdut-military-combination-of-enlisted-and-officers-2010feb22-story.html

Wolfe, R.P. (2011).The New Orleans Lawn Tennis Club: Oldest in the Americas. Multi MediaTechnology Group: South Korea.

4 Governance

Introduction

We are fond of reminding our students that no two clubs are alike. That said, clubs can be similar in certain ways, including the ways in which they are governed. This chapter discusses what governance is, why it is important and presents several different governance models.

What is governance?

Governance is defined as "the process of decision-making and the process by which decisions are implemented (or not implemented)". (https:// en.wikipedia.org/wiki/Good governance). In clubs, this refers to the hierarchy of decision-making, how decisions are made and who makes them. John Kinner, CCM, adds "Governance is the framework, principles, and practices that a club employs to affect decision-making."

In clubs, especially member-owned clubs, many people can be involved in decisions such as whether to embark on a capital project, whether to raise dues, and who to allow in as members. Clubs are complex organizations with a myriad of activities that need to be managed in the club environment.

While there is a large overlap between governance, administration and management, we believe that 'governance' is the preferred term when describing clubs, because of the fact that professional staff (paid) and members (unpaid) work together to make the organization function effectively.

Another way of saying this is that governance is the system used by clubs (and other organizations) to coordinate their activities. Commentators seem to imply that governance occurs only at the highest levels of an organization and is distinguishable from administration and management, which are left to lower echelon employees. However, governance, administration and management are all synonymous. Functionally, it would be challenging to draw lines between governance and administration or management. However, the term 'governance' is normally used when describing how private clubs are formally organized at all levels.

The greatest single driver of club governance is ownership. If a club is a member-owned (equity) club, it is usually operated differently than a club (nonequity) that has a profit or ROI (return on investment) motive.

The type of ownership has a direct correlation to how a particular club is governed and the policies that are created. An example would be a club's dining room operating hours. In an equity club, members can decide to operate the dining room for the convenience of the few members on traditionally slow nights and justify the expenses as shared equally by the entire membership. In contrast, in a nonequity club there would be a high likelihood the dining room would be closed during slack periods for economic reasons. Ownership might then advise the membership that dues might have to be raised to cover the unprofitable hours of operation.

Much of the club management literature to date has focused on and spoken to the operation of equity clubs, as equity clubs have dominated the club industry for many years. As clubs have evolved over the years, however, so too has the popularity of nonequity clubs. In fact, some members of nonequity clubs prefer them because, as members, they are devoid of any governance responsibility (such as serving on committees). They pay their dues and go home after their round of golf or dinner with their families.

Nonequity clubs are governed differently largely because they may have a single owner(s), or a corporate owner. There are even equity clubs that are managed by a management company, which would result in yet another governance model. The purpose of this chapter is to give the student an awareness that the club ownership is key to organizing/governing a club.

Why do organizations need governance?

Organizations have many facets in terms of personnel and activities, too many for any single person to be in all places at all times to ensure that everyone is working towards the same objectives. Governance addresses this problem by establishing a framework in which work can be allocated and coordinated. Furthermore, governance addresses the interaction and division or responsibilities between paid employees and volunteers. This is especially important in equity clubs which depends upon the employees and volunteers (members) working effectively together.

Ray Cronin, of ClubBenchmarking, in an April 7, 2015 presentation to the New Jersey Club Managers Association emphasized the following points about governance:

- Governance is a *process* that must be understood and continuously evolved.
- Governance as *leadership* requires the board to understand the business.
- *Fact-based governance* provides that understanding and a foundation that can transition from board to board.
- Governance as leadership requires the board to focus on what matters – and stay away from what doesn't matter.

Students and managers should appreciate that governance is continually evolving and that the ways in which clubs are governed has changed over the last generation as people, laws and regulations, have changed and new information has emerged.

In addition to ownership, two other primary factors that drive how a club is governed are: (1) its bylaws and (2) its organizational structure. These will be discussed in turn.

Bylaws

The Merriam Webster website (merriam-webster.com/dictionary/bylaw) defines bylaw as: "a rule adopted by an organization chiefly for the government of its members and the regulation of its affairs". Within clubs, bylaws define the rules by which decisions are made and play a critical role in the long-term success of a club.

Bylaws are central to defining and maintaining a club's reason for existence. Bylaws dictate how members are selected; what standing committees exist; how officers are elected; how long their terms are; the different membership categories; rights and privileges of members; when and where annual membership meetings are held; when and where board and committee meetings are held and; how decisions get made.

How are bylaws developed? They can be drawn up by the founders of a club. They can also be copied from like-minded clubs who are anxious to share with fellow clubs. There are also excellent resources available from the National Club Association (NCA; www.nationalclub.org), and the Club Management Association of America (CMAA; www.cmaa.org). Whatever the source, the authors suggest a regular bylaws review by a competent attorney with prior experience in club governance.

One final note about bylaws – our students often confuse bylaws with 'house rules'. Rather than dictate how a club is governed, house rules pertain more to what is allowed and what is not allowed, for instance, how members are expected to dress on the golf course and in the clubhouse; whether or not cell phones are allowed, and, if so, where; where food and beverages may be consumed; and if smoking is allowed. In general, house rules are reviewed (and change) more often than bylaws.

The organizational structure of clubs

Most clubs can be categorized as either equity clubs or nonequity clubs. We will see the governance of equity and nonequity clubs is quite different. Keeping this in mind, the governance model stems largely from the type of club or how they are classified.

As discussed in Chapter 3, clubs may be classified in six different ways:

1 *Ownership* - the club may be owned by a single individual or a group of like-minded individuals.

2 *Tax status* – the club may be organized as non-profit and tax exempt so that operations are conducted to produce break-even operating results.

3 *Clientele* – e.g., the club membership may be limited to property owners in an association, or the club may cater to members of a particular gender, class or ethnicity.

4 *Primary activity/location* – e.g. yacht club, polo club, swim club, golf club, country club.

5 *Size* – categories can include number of members, gross volume or initiation fee. There are clubs with thousands of members, multi-million gross dollar volumes and by comparison, there are clubs with no initiation fees and very modest monthly dues. In most clubs, there is a direct correlation between the size of the club and the number of staff and line employees. The more activities the club supports, the greater the number of committees.

6 *Equity/nonequity* – in an equity club, members may have a portion of the initiation fees returned upon departure from the club. In a nonequity club, any initiation fees are generally not returned.

All of these factors affect the way a cub is governed but we will focus on items 4 and 6 above.

Clubs are generally referred to as either equity or nonequity. Within these broad categories, clubs may also be organized as for-profit or not-for-profit. Generally speaking, equity clubs are those owned by its members and are not-for-profit (and the members own equity in the club). Nonequity clubs are generally owned by an individual or other business entity and are run on a for-profit basis. Some confusion surrounds this distinction, largely because of the initiation fee that members are required to pay upon joining (in both types of clubs). See Exhibit 4.1 below.

Exhibit 4.1: Different ways of classifying a club

In order to operate as a private club, a group of individuals has to organize and operate in accordance with the Federal Tax Code in the USA. Please refer to Exhibit 1.3 (Chapter 1). Organizing in this manner affords the organization tax advantages and other benefits not available to organizations that are open to the general public. Certain tax requirements may be that the club keep records of guest usage (guest book) and that guest usage ($'s) not be greater than 15% of gross sales.

The board of directors

Most equity clubs are not-for-profit and are governed by a board of directors and led by a club president. In many clubs, the directors also serve as liaisons or heads of various standing committees as provided for in the articles of incorporation or by-laws. The number of directors frequently is nine, with one-third of the seats turning over each year.

Directors are usually nominated by a nominating committee that proposes a slate to the general membership. This slate is voted on at the club's annual meeting. The bylaws also stipulate what percentage of votes is needed for approval. In some clubs becoming a director is the first step in a member's advancing through the various positions to the club presidency.

Some clubs may have more than 20 directors and can include past presidents in the board mix. Experienced managers generally agree there is a direct correlation between the size of the governing board and the level of board effectiveness (that is to say, less is more). The Resolve Consulting Group based in Gosford Australia has compiled 12 key characteristics of effective boards as identified by Dr. Robert Andringa, a consultant to Not-for-Profit Boards in the US and around the world. Even though they were written for charities, they apply as well to club boards:

- The board's role is clear and distinct from staff
- The board has a governance focus
- Board members understand their roles
- The board links with 'moral owners' (stakeholders)
- The board adopts clear 'ends' policies (articulated purpose)
- The CEO is the one agent of the board
- Policies are organized in to a board handbook
- The board chair 'manages' the board
- Board committees serve board needs and speak *to* the board not *for* the board
- Board meetings are well planned
- Board members are selected and well orientated
- The board accepts responsibility for improving itself

Source: resolve.consulting/wp-content/uploads/.../027_characteristics-of-an-effective-board.pdf

One of the trends regarding how club boards operate (discussed more fully in Chapter 10) is for boards to professionalize their operations with proper orientation, training, board progression and division of responsibility.

Committee roles and responsibilities

For an equity club to function smoothly and effectively, it must govern with committee roles and responsibilities that are clearly defined and followed by the entire organization. See Exhibits 4.2 and 4.3 below. These should be spelled out in the club's rules and regulations and amended periodically to reflect current practices. Committees may be categorized either as standing committees or ad hoc committees.

Standing committees

Standing committees are usually established in the articles of incorporation and have roles and responsibilities detailed in club rules and regulations. They observe club operations and make recommendations to the board regarding policies and procedures that directly impact member use and financial results.

Standing committees meet on a regular schedule and, in many cases, the chair serves as a director and liaison to the board. Those that are frequently found in private clubs are: Membership, Finance, Greens, Golf, House, Entertainment, Long-Range Planning and Personnel. Depending on the culture of the club, a committee may have the last say on such minor issues as the selection of salt and pepper shakers in the dining room, to more impactful issues such as membership usage of the facilities.

In many clubs, the chairman of the Finance Committee is also a director who serves as treasurer. Frequently the treasurer is a professional accountant who holds a degree in finance and a CPA designation.

Ad hoc committees

Ad hoc committees may be created to address a special issue or project, such as a clubhouse renovation or a streamlining of membership categories. Ad hoc committees make recommendations for board action and approval. Generally, they have no power to sign contracts nor are they able to commit the club to certain courses of action. They serve at the pleasure of the board and are disbanded upon completion of their assigned task. As an example, a club celebrating a 100th anniversary might appoint an ad hoc committee to plan and execute the actual event and still another committee to create a coffee table book memorializing the event.

Club committees, like boards of directors, must operate in a pre-determined manner, with clear objectives, and in adherence to the bylaws. Club Board Professionals in their blog (www.cbpros.com/blog/the-role-of-committees-in-a-private-club) have some excellent insights into committees and governance. Some of the points that they make are that in order to be effective, committees should "be formed at the Board level; the Board and/or Club President should also appoint Committee chairs and approve all committee members" and... "At the very least, a Board member should serve on each committee and facilitate communications with the Board. Board members should also have one or more committee assignments." They go on to suggest that "Committees typically report their activities at each Board meeting. For expediency it is recommended that Committee chairs prepare a brief written report for inclusion in the Board package and that oral reports be limited to items of significance. This will help the Board to focus meetings on strategic and other matters of importance."

A key to good governance is the interaction between the general manager, the board and the committees. Committees work with the board, the management staff, and other constituents to help the club achieve its goals.

General manager

This position is also known as COO in some clubs. The GM/COO looks after the day to day activities while the board focuses on strategy and the longer term (although one trend is seeing the role of the GM expanding into these areas). This individual usually has extensive decision-making autonomy and sets the pace and performance standards of multiple department heads. The GM is broadly charged with the total operation of the club and regularly advising and updating the board and president of operating activities and results. A good way to develop a sense for the complexity of the position and the depth of knowledge required for the position would be to review and compare comprehensive position descriptions which have been developed by various professional organizations such as the Club Management Association of America (CMAA, www.cmaa.org) and the Professional Golfers of America (PGA, www.pga.com).

The responsibilities and authorities of the GM are generally defined by the board and accepted practices. Some managers have the title GM but not the authority. In some clubs, it is the general manager who is the designated point person for initial queries and problem resolution – essentially the club gatekeeper.

The board, committees and general manager operate in consort with each other in achieving the club goals and objectives. There is also a shared vision embraced by the members and the employee group. A strategic plan for the club is key in the achievement of these goals and objectives.

For example: One winter day, a member observes excessive ice buildup on the walkways into the clubhouse. She reports this unsafe condition to the receptionist and the receptionist dispatches a houseman to address the problem with the appropriate sand/salt mixture. The receptionist also advises the GM of the problem and her corrective action. The GM reports the situation to the House Committee chair and includes it in his or her monthly report to the board. And the board may inquire into long term issues/problems associated with the issue.

Chief administrator in the UK

As an aside, sometimes the titles, roles and authority are not always as described above. In the UK (and other Commonwealth countries) the position may also be known as Secretary or Club Secretary. David Roy, Manager of the Crail Golfing Society, suggests that the role of Secretary in the UK has an interesting history. He states that "Originally, golf clubs in the UK were established with a Captain (member) and a Secretary as the sole office bearers.... It would be common for the Secretary to be a solicitor, or local civil servant, with expertise in administration. Thus, the terminology was established very early on. This became more deeply embedded when the legal term 'Company Secretary' was established to refer to the person within a limited company who was legally responsible for filing all the requisite documents with the government (such as the annual statement of accounts)."

He further suggests that recently, "clubs have started to drop the term Club Secretary and refer to the Club Manager. However, this requires a change in mindset from the key influencers in the club. Many club members still consider 'The Committee' as the body that manage their club and their Secretary is simply someone who attends to the administration of the club and has very limited decision making powers."

As the role of GM is changing in North America, so too are the roles of secretary changing in the UK. Mr. Roy concludes by describing the changing conditions: "although the Club Secretary is the most important member of staff in the club, he/she may choose to take a very limited role in the decision making process, abrogating this to the Committee." In such circumstances, the club may have a challenging relationship with the secretary, depending upon expectations. In sum, titles, authority and division of responsibility are changing at some clubs while, at others, the secretary maintains his or her traditional role as an administrator.

Organizational structures of equity clubs

Let's explore some organizational structures commonly associated with equity club operations. Again, ownership drives governance structure. Within the industry, there are a number of club manager governance models which students may observe.

In many clubs, members and directors use the terms GM, Club Manager and Clubhouse Manager almost interchangeably. Some managers and clubs place greater emphasis on titles. For most, the responsibilities and authorities define the position. Exhibits 4.2 and 4.3 below will give the student some ideas as to the various entities, including committees, and roles in club governance as well as the various responsibilities of club governance. Exhibits 4.4 and 4.5 provide additional models that students might see applied in clubs.

Exhibit 4.2: Traditional equity country club governance model (1)

In this model, the responsibilities and authorities of the GM are generally defined by the board and accepted practices, and the superintendent and golf professional report directly to the GM.

In *First Among Equals*, Patrick J. McKenna and David H. Maister argue that fellow professionals can be induced to outperform by inspiration and not by leading or managing them. This triad approach to management also frequently has the GM operating in First Among Equals mode within clubs. This traditional model is found in many clubs is frequently referred to as the Three-Legged Stool and is presented in Exhibit 4.3.

In Model 2, the General Manager has overall responsibility for club operations but leaves the day to day operations of the golf operation and the golf course to the respective professionals. The general manager's direct reports handle the administrative details for the golf professional and superintendent. This would include payroll, health and safety record keeping, vacation computation, employee benefit administration and wage an hour compliance.

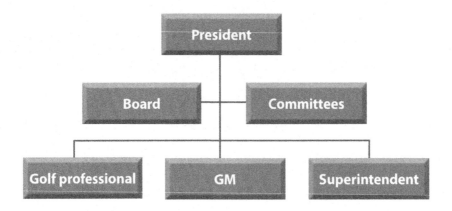

Exhibit 4.3: Traditional equity country club governance model (2)

Club Manager

In yet another model (below) the Club Manager usually has the responsibility of the clubhouse and some additional responsibilities that may include financial reporting, pool operations, tennis operations and other responsibilities as deemed appropriate by the club board. Generally speaking, the country club manager does not get involved with day-to-day operations of the golf operations or the grounds department.

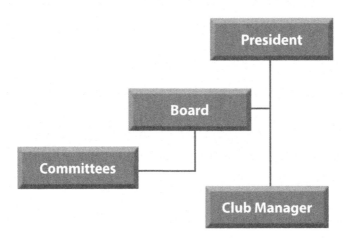

Exhibit 4.4: Club manager model

Clubhouse Manager

It's important to note that the position of Clubhouse Manager, in this model, oversees everything within the confines of the clubhouse. These responsibilities could include food and beverage service and production, building maintenance,

HVAC controls, security and OSHA compliance, but would not include the club's golf operations or grounds department.

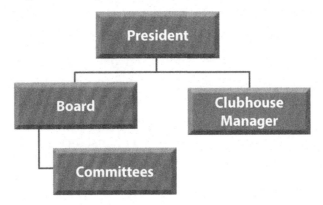

Exhibit. 4.5: Clubhouse Manager

While there is no 'correct' model, and some models work better in some contexts, a trend in the industry is for the general manager to take on more of a COO role, working directly with the board and seeing the superintendent and the director of golf reporting to the GM.

The organizational structure of nonequity clubs

Governance

Governance in a nonequity club is at the discretion of the owner or owners. Clubs must also follow state and federal regulations, but rules, regulations and operating philosophies are within the purview of the owner(s). Execution of the owner's operating philosophies is usually left to the GM.

In many nonequity clubs, standing or ad-hoc committees are non-existent. However, advisory committees may be organized by the owner. The role of the advisory committee in a nonequity club may provide an excellent venue for thoughtful suggestions and recommendation by the membership.

The admissions decision in nonequity clubs is frequently made by either the manager or the membership director. Then, the paperwork/logistics would be handled by a membership secretary or director of membership.

In an equity club however, there is usually an admission process that may include sponsors, a formal application, vetting by an admissions committee, a meet and greet cocktail party, member recommendations, posting of the applicant to the general membership, and a decision.

Management companies

Clubs may be individually owned, or part of an organization that develops, operates, owns and/or manages facilities regionally, nationally or even internationally. In these governance is administered or orchestrated through centralized decision making. This centralized decision making provides clear definitions of roles, responsibilities and expected results across the organization. These clubs frequently have reciprocal agreements so that members of one club may use the facilities of an affiliated club. The members enjoy signing privileges and have charges billed to their home club. For instance, many city clubs have sleeping rooms available to members and reciprocal members.

From the member perspective, there may be many benefits to membership in a a club that is part of a club management group. The benefits can include a membership experience that is consistent, dues levels that are competitive in the marketplace and a significantly reduced need for member involvement in club administration. For some members, however, the corporate approach to bottom line results may be a turnoff.

Over the years, corporate club companies, such as ClubCorp (www.clubcorp.com), have purchased clubs and operated them as for-profit. Currently, ClubCorp owns or operates a portfolio of more than 200 golf and country clubs, business clubs, sports clubs and alumni clubs in 26 states, the District of Columbia and three countries. They have a market capitalization of $1 billion and 65 million shares issued and outstanding. ClubCorp went private in 2017.

Management companies, such as Troon (www.troongolf.com), also manage their own clubs and operate private equity clubs. Troon is privately held; the estimated revenues are $236 million and they have over 240 clubs under contract. They currently manage the links at more than 110 golf courses throughout the US and in about 25 other countries, including the United Arab Emirates, Fiji, and St. Lucia. The company offers its management clients design and development services, payroll and human resources, agronomy, sales and marketing, and food and beverage operations. Troon Privé is its special division dedicated to serving private golf clubs; in addition, Troon Golf offers golf vacation packages and it operates golf schools. According to *Golf Inc.* magazine, the largest management companies (as of 2018) include: Troon (USA); ClubCorp (USA); Accordia Golf Company (Japan); Billy Caspar Golf (USA); Pacific Golf Management (Japan) and KemperSports (USA). Bluegreen and UGOLF are the two largest golf management companies in Europe. Keep in mind that some of these companies operate public resorts in addition to private clubs.

In a nonequity club, the owner determines the club culture and direction, and has the final say in operational decisions. The owner may delegate some decision-making authority to managers or department heads. When advisory committees exist, they generally have limited power and are truly advisory.

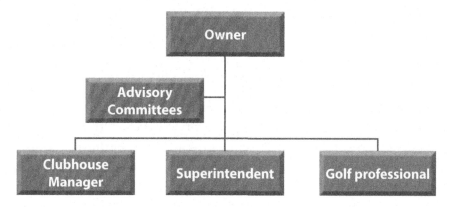

Exhibit 4.6: Nonequity club governance model

City club governance model

City club governance can run the gamut of complexity and extensive member involvement. In smaller city clubs (equity) the general manager may have great latitude in club operations and make many decisions without consultation of club officers or committee chairs.

In larger clubs there may be extensive board and committee involvement because the club has thousands of members and committees operate like de facto clubs within a club. Some of the larger clubs may have committees that oversee areas like specific racquet sports such as squash. The committee may be involved in court scheduling, hiring a professional, court maintenance, competitions, committee communications, member dissatisfactions and capital improvements.

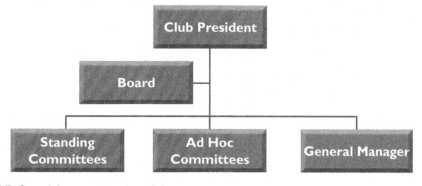

Exhibit 4.7: City club governance model

City clubs can also have such diverse activities as theatre club, cardio rehab, wine club, bridge club and travel club. The possibilities are endless. The level of interaction and involvement between management and committee chairs is usually set by the wants and needs of the particular committee chair. Exhibit 4.7 shows one example of a city club organization chart.

Yacht club governance model

To the uninitiated, yacht club governance could seem mildly peculiar or even a throwback to early naval military history. However, there is a method to the madness. By the nature of most yacht clubs and their enthusiastic supporters, member participation is generally at a higher and more direct level. Many yacht clubs have work parties where members participate, installing docks, giving facilities a fresh coat of paint or combing the club beach for litter. There is a camaraderie and sense of family that is not necessarily experienced in other types of clubs.

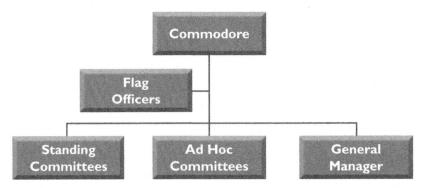

Exhibit 4.8: Yacht club governance model

Yacht clubs can have great diversity in the types of positions that are required at a busy club. These can include: dockmaster, harbormaster, tender or launch manager, pool director, beach managers, sailing instructor, food and beverage manager and catering director.

Summary

In this chapter we have defined governance and explained that ownership, bylaws and organizational structure dictate the club governance. We have looked at club classifications and the various organizational structures in equity and nonequity clubs. We have also discussed managed clubs.

Frequently industry professionals are terrific resources, and club management is no exception. John Kinner, CCM, (quoted earlier in the chapter) is president of Private Club Governance and was a manager in the industry for 35 years. He has a wealth of expertise in the area of club governance and has lectured many times to fellow professionals and club boards. He provides some final thoughts:

- Clubs differ from hotels, restaurants, and other hospitality establishments primarily in the way they are governed. To understand clubs, one must understand governance.

- The practice of sound governance is the single most important controllable factor that will determine the level of success that any club achieves.

Discussion questions

1 Identify the oldest local country club in your area and create an organization chart of that club. Compare it to the newest country club in your area. What are the major differences and similarities?

2 Identify a large city club nearby. What services do the offer and why? How does this compare to the amenities offered by a local country club of your choice? And how is management of the various activities organized?

3 Working with committees in any type of club can be a challenge. If you were coming in to a club as a new manager what would your strategy for success be?

References

Club Board Professionals, www.cbpros.com/blog/the-role-of-committees-in-a-private-club

Merriam-Webster, www.merriam-webster.com/dictionary/bylaw

Resolve Consulting, resolve.consulting/wp-content/uploads/.../027_characteristics-of-an-effective-board.pdf

Wikipedia, https://en.wikipedia.org/wiki/ Good governance

5 People in Clubs

Introduction

In this chapter, we will look at some of the functions of Human Resources Management (HRM) in private clubs. Human resource management encompasses the range of functions which impact employees from recruiting and hiring, to the structure of jobs, to training and development, to performance evaluations and rewards. It also includes administration of employee benefits, salary determination, promotions and transfers, and looking after employee health and safety. And more! It is not the intent of this chapter to provide a comprehensive HRM primer, but rather to provide a snapshot of HRM practices that managers and clubs find useful in day-to-day operations. First, though, we will examine how the management of human resources in clubs is different than it is in other types of hospitality organizations.

Why clubs are different

The management of human resources is different in the hospitality industry than in other industries. Perhaps the primary reason for this is the fact that the hospitality industry is labour-intensive. That is, it simply requires a larger number of employees to perform a job (and interact with customers) than is true in other industries. The club industry is similar, only more so because of members' expectations that their club is a home away from home – and this requires a high degree of personal attention by a club's employees. The member expectations might include name recognition, preferential and deferential treatment, along with generous amounts of perceived value for the dues dollar. From the HRM perspective, it takes special people to provide this level of member service. One important group of club employees are its hourly workers. As a result, the proper recruitment of employees or "putting the right people in the right jobs" is paramount. Since the bulk of employees in clubs are hourly staff, we will begin with an overview of hourly workers.

Hourly workers

Hourly workers are at the heart of what clubs offer and they are critical to its success. They include food and beverage servers, bartenders, grounds crew, maintenance workers, housekeepers, etc. In order to attract these types of workers, especially during periods of low unemployment, clubs must present themselves to be employers of choice. There are a number of factors that hourly workers would find desirable about working in a club, which clubs should leverage. These may include: compensation, seasonality, work environment, benefits, and the potential of housing.

Compensation

For hourly employees, compensation in clubs is usually competitive, but may not greatly exceed market averages. Most employees enjoy a strong base hourly wage. However, clubs will often find themselves in competition for the same employees with employers from the hotel, restaurant, casino and retail industries. This is particularly for food servers, bartenders and cooks.

In the case of food servers, unlike in the commercial sector, there is usually no tipping. Rather, a service charge is added to the bill (something between 18% and 20%). This charge is usually distributed by formula to those working a particular shift or event. Additionally, a club may be structured to provide a holiday or season end bonus.

Tipping, service charges, or club charges can be a source of problems and even litigation. In one instance, a club was ordered to pay $4 million to employees who claimed the 'Club Charge' was collected in lieu of a gratuity. The lesson here is that if members are charged a surcharge on food and beverage, and if it is not directly dispersed to employees, this should be made clear to members.

The main point here is that in most clubs, tipping is not allowed, but service staff receive a higher than average hourly wage, regardless of the origin of the funds used for this compensation. Some employees are attracted by this and others, who are driven by tips, are not.

Clubs that are able to be creative in the area of employee compensation and benefits frequently enjoy a level of staff loyalty that does not usually exist in the commercial hospitality sector. In many clubs, longevity is rewarded with job stability. Long-tenured employees may be considered family. The work environment of a club is one where, very often, luxury and plush surrounding go hand in hand. The work is frequently at a relaxed efficient pace where members are respected, and very high levels of individual attention are provided.

Work environment

Another aspect of clubs that hourly employees might find desirable is the work environment. There are a variety of factors that make the private club work environment different and desirable. Clubs are often housed in majestic buildings (not unlike a luxury hotel), or on expansive grounds. The combination of the physical environment and the familiarity create a positive environment. Hours may not be as long either, as clubs are not open for the same duration as commercial operations. They are also typically closed for one day a week, giving everyone a legitimate day off.

Seasonality

Many clubs are seasonal, and this is particularly true in both the colder and warmer parts of the world. For seasonal clubs, it is like starting a new operation every year with many new hires – much like a resort. While managing a seasonal operation can be challenging for managers, seasonal employment may be very desirable for some employees. It gives them a chance to work in two (or sometimes more) different parts of the country or the world, in different environments. It also gives them the opportunity for a variety of work environments, which can reduce monotony and boredom.

Perks

A distinct plus for golf enthusiasts is that many clubs allow staff to play golf on Mondays when clubs are frequently closed. In some clubs this privilege may be extended to tennis facilities and even health fitness facilities.

Housing

Some clubs provide housing, particularly those which recruit seasonal staff and are located in expensive/resort areas. Again, this can serve as an attractive attribute if offered and may be a deterrent if it is not available.

In summing up why working in clubs is different and why hourly employees are so important, we like this quote from the National Club Association (HR Management: Best Practices for Private Clubs, 2013).

"Clubs, to a very large extent, are only as good as the membership, the facilities and the staff. The quality of life at a club enhances the desirability of membership and social standing. Clubs that consistently provide a cordial, welcoming environment are actively sought out by potential members and employees."

With so many employees (even medium sized clubs may employ over 100 employees), clubs must have human resource policies and procedures in place, systems for paying people and resources to leverage when human resource problems arise. In other words, human resources must be planned for and actively managed.

Who manages Human Resources?

In clubs which have someone in the position of Human Resource Director (HRD), the HRD would be responsible for establishing policies and procedures, overseeing all human resource activities, and advocating for employees. They would also be knowledgeable about HR law (such as wage and hour laws, health and safety and sexual harassment). The authors' research has found that key drivers in the club's decision to have a formal HRD (and/or department) are: size of the employee group, direct costs and seasonality.

However, in many clubs there is no Human Resources Director (HRD). This, again, makes it different than many hotels and restaurants. Not having human resource directors (or a single person in charge) is largely the result of tradition, costs, and the small scale of most clubs. As a manager or supervisor, you would be responsible for negotiating the responsibilities of a mix of hourly employees, other managerial staff and independent contractors. Where there is no HRD, human resource functions are dispersed.

HR delivery in clubs

In the absence of an HRD, the delivery methods of human resources management (who does what) vary from club to club. The basics, such as payroll, benefits administration, tax compliance, wage and hour, and health and safety compliance must ultimately be delivered by all clubs, no matter who does it.

One of the major factors that determine whether a club has an HRD is the size of the club. Size is often based upon the number of members, revenue, or number of employees. Most of the clubs with which we have interacted range in size from about 300 to about 1,000 members (although some clubs can be much smaller or larger). Clubs in this range typically employ between 50 to 150, in season, and would generate between $3 million USD and $12 million USD. Research has shown that clubs begin to consider hiring a HRD when they reach 700 members or about 150 employees.

Some of the other factors that impact delivery methods include: size and skill level of office staff, skills of department heads, technology, complexity of the regulatory environment, number of hourly vs salary employees (exempt vs non-exempt), available resources, seasonality of club operations, and whether the club is an independent or part of a corporation.

In the corporate club environment, the HRM function may be centralized in a home office with operational data and personnel records entered remotely by club employees. Payrolls are generated remotely, and direct deposit is promoted as an employee benefit.

In independent clubs (whether equity or nonequity) managing human resources can be more challenging. Depending on the size of the club and available resources, HR responsibilities can be handled by a HR department, HR staffer, accounting staff, payroll clerk, department heads, assistant manager or GM (or some combination). Very frequently, the administrative function is shared among several individuals within the organization, for instance, payroll may be managed in the accounting office.

The club may also call on outside counsel or an HR consultant for particularly thorny situations that may recall legal assistance. Indeed, one of the trends in clubs is to outsource some HR tasks, which can help clubs and club managers focus on their core competencies.

Outsourcing

Outsourcing the HR function was not even a consideration for many clubs, even just a few years ago. The club operations were considered sacrosanct and outsiders were not to be privy to the inner workings of the club. However, clubs slowly turned to partial outsourcing by first using payroll companies. The payroll companies ultimately morphed into off-site human resource vendors. One such company is Oasis Outsourcing, a national company (USA) which offers human resources support. According to their web site: "Oasis Outsourcing is one of the nation's largest Professional Employer Organizations (PEOs) providing Human Resources Services, Employee Benefits, Healthcare Reform Support, Payroll Administration, and Risk Management Services to clients nationwide. As a PEO, we offer businesses comprehensive human resources support with products and services that can cut administrative costs, reduce liabilities and enhance employee benefits." (https://www.oasisadvantage.com). According to Rachel Barden, Professional Employer Consultant for the company, Oasis helps clubs with a variety of services as an 'administrative employer' or 'co-employer'. Specifically, they can help a club manage its payroll, benefits, risk management programmes, and other human resource related functions (such as infrastructure development and compliance assistance). Rachel suggests that outsourcing in clubs (as well as other industries) is growing as the regulatory environment becomes more complex.

Some club managers and clubs have come to realize that the HR complexities are best dealt with by professional HR companies, such as Oasis. Other companies, such as ADP, Insperity HR Services and many others offer HR solutions that include payroll, new applicant tracking, employee scheduling, performance appraisal and talent management. A large consideration of outsourcing is the cost/benefit. Ultimately, the GM is responsible for ensuring that the HR function operates correctly.

The fact remains that, in many clubs, outsourced functions are primarily back-of-the-house functions, such as payroll. Most clubs continue to manage most other HR functions, including recruiting and hiring, except for management and independent contractors, which are discussed later in the chapter. Other functions, such as training, may be managed both in-house and outsourced.

Recruiting and hiring in clubs

Recruitment is the first step in the employee placement process. According to Christiansen Hughes (2002), recruitment is defined as: "the process of attracting a pool of qualified job candidates from which the organization may select appropriate individuals to meet its job requirements" (pp. 17).

Clubs recruit differently than do other organizations. Except in the largest of clubs (which commonly employ human resource directors), the recruitment and hiring responsibilities are delegated throughout the club, and particularly to managers and department heads. With the advent of the internet and social media, clubs can advertise for positions on the same day there is an opening.

Recruiting is the key to quality hiring. Clubs use a variety of sites to recruit employees including: Monster.com, Indeed, HRCareers, craigslist.com, LinkedIn, college websites, executive placement, the Club Management Association of America (CMAA) website, and regional chapter websites. For instance, the website for the New England Club Managers Association has three separate career sections: one for general managers, one for other management positions, and one for students' jobs and internships.

Clubs also seem to be utilizing their own websites more as a means of recruiting. Not only are they able to promote themselves by featuring attractive photo montages, they are also able to share testimonials by satisfied employees and key staff. Some clubs have separate tabs for Careers and Employment, such as the New York Athletic Club, The Arts Club (London), and the Union League of Chicago.

The draw of additional perquisites to potential hires cannot be over-emphasized (as previously mentioned, use of golf facilities on slow days or when the clubs is normally closed). An active caddy program can provide lucrative seasonal employment. The caddy program may also have a scholarship component. And last, but not least, member relationships and quality of work life are a large draw for many potential employees.

Work visa programmes are also critical for clubs which recruit internationally. These provide excellent earning and learning opportunities for international students. The club may also have a sister club where work exchange positions are rotated through the organization.

Salaried employees and independent contractors

Recruiting for these employees can be different than recruiting for hourly employees. Much recruiting is done via word of mouth, hiring specialists or through professional associations, such as the CMAA, the Golf Course Superintendents Association or the Club Managers Association of Europe. Managers might also be recruited through executive recruiters. One of the authors was an executive recruiter for many years and placed many club managers in jobs throughout the USA.

Independent contractor (golf and tennis professionals) leads could be developed through club member referrals and trade associations. In many cases, word of mouth or employee referrals fill the job opening.

Screening and selection

Once recruiting is complete, clubs are able to collect and partially process applications from interested applicants. Additionally, if authorized, they can (and should) run extensive background checks as part of the pre-employment screening process. This may include: local criminal, national criminal, Department of Motor Vehicles (or Driver and Vehicle Agency, etc.), Sexual Predator Data Base, credit check, Facebook, Google, Social Security (or similar), Trace, educational credentials, drug screen and personality profile. It should be noted that state and federal laws must always be observed so as to avoid legal issues over hiring or termination policies and procedures. Additional checks will be necessary if the candidate will be working with children, such as at the pool or with camps or clinics.

When hiring a general manager there is usually a search committee which recommends a candidate to the board. The search committee is comprised of key board members and committee chairs. Frequently an executive recruiter will be retained to assist the club in evaluating and recommending qualified candidates for the position.

In the hiring of department heads such as a golf professional or superintendent there is usually a formal search committee headed by a board chair. The general manager is very involved in the process. For lesser department heads, such as a food and beverage manager a committee chair and general manager may conduct the search in conjunction with members of the house committee.

After potential hires are suitably screened then selection and final selection can begin in earnest. The interview process should be structured and consistent. There are reams and reams of published information on interview techniques and questions. These authors suggest avoiding 'warm body' hires ('any one will do') whenever possible. Additionally, having a probationary period as part of the hiring procedures is strongly recommended.

Independent contractors

Historically, several positions in clubs have been hired as what are known as independent contractors, primarily: golf and tennis professionals and; caddies. Being an independent contractor means that the job incumbent is paid a salary and has a certain level of autonomy. It also dictates what benefits the club will provide (or not). Teaching professional and the golf professional independent contractor status has been debated for decades. In the USA, In the Department of Labor and the Internal Revenue Service have become involved. There seem to be fewer and fewer reasons to not classify these individuals as salaried employees. This trend can also impact assistant golf professionals and tennis professionals.

This has become such an important topic that both Professional Golfers Association (PGA: www.pga.org) and the National Golf Course Owners Association (NGCOA: www. ngcoa.org) have taken positions on it. The PGA advises its members that the Department of Labor considers most golf professionals to be employees, rather than independent contractors. NCGOA advises members that if a golf professional is found by the Department of Labor to be an employee rather than an independent contractor there can be far reaching financial ramifications.

Even though the use of caddies has decreased in many countries, there are still questions around their status. Do caddies have independent contractor status? The debate continues regarding their status due to the myriad legal opinions on the state and federal levels. It is recommended that clubs consult local laws and regulations.

To summarize, many positions have historically been hired as independent contractors (Uber drivers are the latest example) but the courts are questioning what an independent contractor is and is not. The Department of Labor and the Internal Revenue Service have tests for positions. It is called the 'economic realities test' and is comprised of six questions:

1   Is the work an integral part of the business?
2   Does the worker's managerial skill affect his or her profit or loss?
3   How does the worker's investment compare to the employer's investment?
4   Does the work require special skill and initiative?
5   Is the relationship indefinite?
6   What is the nature and degree of the employer's control?

The authors suggest that in the area HR administration of independent contractors, clubs can never receive too much advice from experienced labour counsel. A long, drawn-out contestment with federal or state authorities is likely to be expensive and potentially demoralizing to the employee in question.

Salaried employees

Unlike hourly employees, salaried employees are hired by the club to perform a specific task for a set rate of compensation. These employees usually work the number of hours, shifts or days that are required to complete the assigned tasks. Examples of salaried employees in a club could include: general manager (previously discussed), assistant general manager (or clubhouse manager), dockmaster, comptroller, executive chef and golf course superintendent. Most salaried employees are exempt from overtime regulations.

Jobs and job descriptions

What is a job description? Cole (2002) has defined a job description as "A statement of overall purpose and scope of a job, together with the details of its tasks and duties..."

The term *job description* can be associated with other terms including job specification, job duties, job responsibilities and others. The Society of Human Resource Management (SHRM) www.shrm.org is an excellent resource for those seeking additional insights into job descriptions. Where do you find them for the multitude of positions in clubs? A great resource for club management related jobs and job descriptions is the CMAA website www.cmaa.org. Similarly, the Professional Golfers of America (www.pga.org) and Golf Course Superintendents Association (www.gcsaa.org) have copious amounts of job related information.

Google searches will reveal executive search firms, clubs looking for managers, international management openings and real-estate developers seeking Community Association Managers (CAMs) and Golf Resort Managers. Each of these opportunities will have a detailed job description and should have a list of job expectations.

Job descriptions are important for the employer and the job incumbent. The employer is able to set forth expectations for the position, areas of responsibility, etc. The job incumbent can get a sense what is expected and the demands of the job. Job descriptions are important for all jobs, not just some. They are critical in areas such as preventing lawsuits, for wage and benefit entitlements and promotions (when tied to performance evaluations). Retirement benefits may be impacted by responsibilities and authorities, and defined in initial and subsequent performance evaluations.

It is important for managers to be aware of certain key definitions within the HR domain. Students should recognize and be able to differentiate between 'job descriptions' which list the duties associated with the job and 'job qualifications' or 'job specifications' which refer to the education, work experience, and skills appearing on a job opening.

Continuing professional development

Continuing professional development is a concept that the authors strongly support. Even though an individual may have a hospitality management degree, keeping abreast of industry trends and shifts in the marketplace is essential to remaining current and relevant to their club, club members and employees. As a manager, you will want to have the active support of your club with membership and/or participation in professional organizations such as the Professional Golfers' Association (PGA), Club Management Association of America (CMAA), Club Management Association of Europe (CMAE), Professional Club Marketing Association (PCMA), Golf Course Superintendents Association (GCSA), US Professional Tennis Association (USPTA), etc.

Keep in mind that clubs are different (as we keep reminding you). This is especially true when it comes to professional development. Many students who enter the hospitality industry will take jobs in hotels and restaurants, many of which are a part of larger chains. Large chains are able to provide professional development opportunities to their employees because of their economies of scale. Most clubs, however, are smaller, independent operations. Because of this, they do not have the same ability to provide professional development opportunities themselves.

That is why clubs, and their employees, depend largely upon professional associations for professional development. This is true for managers, superintendents and golf/tennis/fitness professionals.

The CMAA, as well as CMAE and others, are very focused on the professional development of their members. Within the associations, the chapters are encouraged to implement education programs at the local level. Chapter members are encouraged have key staff attend local meetings.

On a national level, CMAA conducts a Leadership Conference for chapter officers as well as Business Management Institutes (BMIs) for aspiring managers. CMAA also encourages professional development through a credentialing program to certify club managers as Certified Club Managers (CCM) and Master Club Managers (MCM). These credentials have extensive educational, CMAA activity and community service components.

And professional development habits begin early, while enrolled in educational programmes. We strongly encourage students to enhance their learning 'beyond the classroom', by joining student chapters of professional organizations, conducting site visits and having informational interviews with managers.

Strategic career advancement is a hallmark of the professional manager. Advancing through the ranks as a professional manager generally requires lateral and upward moves to larger and more complex operations over time. For assistant managers, many general managers subscribe to the 'Three-Year Rule' and expect their assistant manager to acquire their own club or additional experience in a different club setting.

Best practices for developing an HR strategy

Just as it is important to have a general business strategy in order to run an effective business, it is equally important to have a HR strategy in a club. This will allow the club to treat people fairly, pay people fairly, encourage and develop employees, manage within the law, deliver high levels of member service and satisfaction, and to become and remain an employer of choice.

An HR strategy is an overarching plan that allows a company to establish a club culture, create a sense of a team with a single direction, allows for transparent communication and provides the proper tools for employees to do their jobs. Human resource strategy also assures that employees meet the goals, mission and future needs of the company.

Angela Sarver (a financial advisor) suggests 10 best practices for developing a human resource strategy within an organization. Even though they were written for financial advisers, they apply as well to club operations.

1 "Differentiate your business to recruit the best people.

2 Recruit for skill and cultural fit.

3 Define expectations.

4 Provide regular feedback.

5 Learn what motivates employees.

6 Delegate.

7 Embrace technology.

8 Invest in staff development.

9 Clearly communicate your compensation program.

10 Be accessible."

Source: https://blog.commonwealth.com/10-best-practices-for-developing-a-human-resources-strategy

Summary

HRM seems to finally be recognized as critical to organizational success within clubs. After all, clubs are only as good as their staffs. The National Club Association in their publication *HR Management, Best Practices for Private Clubs* makes the case that strategic HR management is critical to clubs and that time and resources dedicated to this aspect of private club operations are key to a club's success. We are not sure which comes first, making the time or securing the resources for a HR strategic plan, but we heartily endorse the concept. Employees must have a solid, reliable base from which to operate. Club cultures going forward need to embrace HR concepts, solutions and strategies that enhance the member and staff experience. In the final analysis, private clubs are only as good as their staffs.

The HRM function within an organization has to make the 'trains run on time.' HR functions such as training and development, compensation, benefits, labor relations, staffing, and performance management should function seamlessly. In addition, business knowledge is critical to HRM success. This includes operations knowledge, financial acumen, customer knowledge, competitors and partners, to name a few.

With the HRM functions performing, and a solid mastery of the business areas previously mentioned, the HRM staff will be able to develop the internal consulting skills that will make it a strategic business partner and change agent. Lastly, ideally the HRM function should be overseen by a knowledgeable professional.

Discussion questions

1   Identify the most prevalent HR models in your local clubs? What are the differences among them? What are the managerial implications?

2   Create a flow chart of the hourly employee hiring processes from application to orientation.

3   How much time do area club managers spend on HR related tasks? Are they considering outsourcing any of these tasks of job functions? Are there overlapping responsibilities in the HR department?

4   What do your area club managers consider their greatest HRM challenges?

References

Cole, G. (2002). *Personnel and Human Resource Management*. Continuum: London.

Hughes, J.M.C. (2002). 'Recruitment and selection issues and strategies within international resort communities', in *Resourcing in Human Resource Management*. N. D'Annunzio-Green, G. Maxwell & S. Watson (Eds.). Continuum: London.

National Club Association (2013). *HR Management: Best Practices for Private Clubs*. Washington, DC: NCA

Oasis Advantage (n.d.). https://www.oasisadvantage.com/

Sarver, A. (n.d.). https://blog.commonwealth.com/10-best-practices-for -developing-a-human-resources-strategy

6 Food and Beverage

Introduction

Many club managers would agree that comparing commercial food and beverage operations to private clubs is like comparing apples to oranges. Clubs are uniquely challenged with multiple dining options (much like a hotel or resort) and in the ability to forecast demand, because many members may not make reservations. Additionally, many club food and beverage operations lose money because of high food and labor costs (more will be said about this later). Finally, club dining is reserved for members only, so clubs are serving a limited market. There are other differences, but these are some of the key ones, all of which present unique challenges. According to research by ClubBenchmarking, 75% of food and beverage departments in clubs lose money. This is not necessarily a good or a bad thing – just a function of how food and beverage in clubs is managed. This chapter will explain how they are managed, how they are similar to (and different from) restaurants, and why so many of them lose money or show a deficit. We will revisit these issues but, first, let's confirm how important food and beverage is to a club's livelihood.

Dining has been an important part of clubs (all types) for a very long time. Dining clubs in the US, such as the Wednesday Evening Club (Boston), date from the 1700s. Later, the Thursday Evening Club and the Saturday Club served the same purpose of allowing limited numbers of men to dine together in various restaurants, hotels or even other clubs. While most of these clubs had no permanent home, they served many of the same needs as today's clubs do by providing food, drink, and comradery in a social setting. The differences between then and now are significant, however. A once a week, or once a month, dinner was easily paid for, especially if using someone else's facility. The evening bill was divided up, each member paid their share and that was that. Today, when a club operates its own facility, or facilities, accommodates hundreds or thousands of members, and hires staff to prepare and serve the food, the economies of scale change dramatically. Much of this chapter is focused on how such operations are managed.

Importance of food and beverage to clubs

To many members, food and beverage offerings in a club are the lifeblood of the club – that is the primary reason to be at the club day in and day out (in addition to socializing with the other members). It has been suggested that food and beverage: (1) helps to attract new members; (2) contributes to member satisfaction; and (3) helps achieve financial objectives (Barrows, 1997). To elaborate, a person's first exposure to a club may very well be as a guest of a member at a meal or event (which would typically include food). In fact, many clubs host annual Member/Guest golf tournaments and events which go a long way in introducing the club to nonmembers. In instances such as these, food and beverage becomes the face of the club – that is, impressions are made based upon the quality of the experience. If it is positive, it may result in the guest wanting to join the club as a member.

Second, surveys of members consistently indicate that food and beverage is a factor in their overall satisfaction at their clubs. That also speaks to the importance of providing a quality experience day in and day out. Otherwise, it could result in the loss of a member.

Finally, although many food and beverage departments lose money, they generate revenues that are important to club operations – and are often the second greatest source of revenues (after dues).

Photo 6.1: The Harvard Club – a dining room. Courtesy of the Harvard Club of Boston

But, in order to attract new members, satisfy current members and generate revenues, food and beverage programmes require a high level of expertise, creativity and attention to detail. When all of these elements are combined, both organizational objectives and members expectations are met.

Members appreciate many aspects of dining at their clubs (as opposed to a local restaurant or at home). These include: not always having to make reservations, being greeted by name at the door, getting their favourite table, being assigned to their favourite server, having a staff member who knows their likes and dislikes, seeing familiar faces in the clubhouse and dining room, being able to order what they want, receiving an alcoholic beverage with a generous pour and not having to tip! Such are the benefits of membership at a private club. But this all comes at a price, as will be discussed.

Who runs the department?

Like other departments, staffing and authority is largely contingent upon the size of the department. In very small clubs (yacht, city or country), the club manager may oversee day-to-day F & B operations in the club. In larger (country) clubs, the clubhouse manager may have responsibility for all operations in the clubhouse, including F & B. If the club is large enough, there may be a dedicated director of food and beverage. Also, in larger clubs, there will be 'outlet' managers, for individual dining rooms, and other larger satellite operations. There is usually a separate manager for events, discussed below.

Characteristics of food and beverage operations

For those students who are familiar with restaurants (having owned one, worked in one, or eaten in one), they will note that club food and beverage operations have some similarities with commercial restaurants. On the surface, clubs provide food and drinks (alcoholic and non); table service; banquets and catering; accommodation for special events; and they charge money for such services. Also, like restaurants, they must be responsive to their markets; menus must be developed that will be desirable; they are labour intensive; and place an emphasis on quality.

It is here that the differences begin and end. Unlike restaurants, they provide multiple outlets (similar to hotels and resorts), varying levels of service (which can create challenges), must meet special needs of members and host many special events, themes, etc. Finally, members have input into food and beverage operations (via the House Committee). Imagine if regular customers in restaurants had decision making authority!

We will talk about some of the key characteristics of food and beverage from the member's perspective, from a profitability perspective, and from an operational perspective.

Country club members' perspective

Let us start at the beginning though, by stating that almost every club has some form of food and beverage operation, however modest it may be. This includes city clubs, country clubs, racquet clubs, yacht clubs and all others that we have discussed. In fact, arguably, it is the one amenity that all clubs have in common. Some operations may consist of nothing more than a snack bar while others will offer sit-down, full-service restaurant operations. In fact, many clubs offer a range and combination of operations and the larger they are, the more options they typically provide. Some even provide food trucks! Let's examine some of the unique characteristics of club dining.

First, clubs offer food and beverage to their members only, except where they allow nonmember events, which will be discussed later. Even if an operation calls itself a club, but opens its dining room to the public, chances are it is not a true private club. For private clubs, servicing members only, this means that management and service staff see members often (sometimes every day), get to know their likes and dislikes, know where they like to sit in the dining room, get to know their families, etc. Inside the clubhouse, the dining room is where members and staff come to know one another best. Remember that most members eating a meal at their club have many other options. By being there, they are forgoing eating in the hip new restaurant in town or any of the other restaurants that they may be curious about. In fact, the dining experience that they have at their club is the exact opposite of 'curious'. They are eating there for the sense of familiarity, because they are known and they will be taken care of. In short, they expect that there will be no surprises. They may sit at the same table every time (and even the same seat), request the same server and order the same food. Management must recognize this, expect it and act accordingly.

Members may feel so comfortable at their club that they may not make reservations, even when they are requested. This can make it difficult to forecast demand and put unnecessary pressures on the kitchen and dining room. This is illustrated in the following example.

Exhibit 6.1: Members are creatures of habit

Members can be creatures of habit – the reference to sitting at the same table and seat is no joke. One of the authors worked at a private club which still had a formal dining room at the time. The dining room overlooked the golf course, as many do, and two tables in particular (Tables # 5 and # 6) had spectacular views. One couple always came in for Sunday brunch and requested Table 6. Another couple ate at the club every Tuesday night and requested Table 6. This was not a problem and we were always able to accommodate them. Until the time that they both came in (unexpectedly) on a Wednesday night, at the same time, requesting the same table. We should add that the two couples did not like each other so sitting them together at the same table was not an option. What would you do?

Members may also bring guests (family, friends, or business associates), which is generally allowed at most clubs. When members bring guests to their club, it can be a very symbolic gesture. It might mean that 'you are a member of our family'; it may be a special occasion; or they simply might be trying to impress. Whatever the reason, certain protocols are in order when guests are present. Familiarity may take precedence; members might expect an added degree of deference; or they might just be showing off. Other protocols may involve who sits where, who gets which menu and whether a visit by the general manager or a board member has been pre-arranged. Some clubs still have two types of menus – one with prices and one without. In these clubs, upon request, the host may be the only person who sees the menu prices.

Members also have choices once they arrive at the club. For instance, a 1,000-member full-service country club might offer two, or even three dining rooms, a banquet department with multiple function rooms, a snack bar by the pool, some sort of food service operation on the golf course and a bar. Food and drink might be available for the entire time that the club is open, beginning with breakfast and ending with dinner in the dining rooms. Further, club members may be allowed to order off a variety of menus. Many clubs will have different menus for different dining areas but, at the same time, allow members to order off the menu of their choice.

This is an important point to make – that members receive deferential treatment. After all, at least in member-owned clubs, they are the owners. It can be difficult, if not a bad idea, to say 'no' to a member. Within reason, they should be able to come when they want to, eat where they want to, sit where they want to and get what they want. This is what they are paying for as members.

City club members' perspective

Compared with country clubs, discussed above, a city club of about the same size might offer multiple dining spaces, depending upon the layout and configuration of the building. They might provide anything from coffee and pastries to a full breakfast in the morning. Breakfast is a particularly important meal, especially for clubs that have overnight guest rooms. Also, for those clubs that allow business to be conducted on the premises (not all do), breakfast can be a good time for business meetings to take place. City clubs will also offer lunch, which would be the busiest meal period because of business people working in the area. And the club might offer dinner, if not every night, then as many as five nights a week.

Some city clubs have extensive banquet facilities, ballrooms, and private dining spaces for members. Some city clubs have expansive bars as well, which can be the most active and popular spaces in the entire club. One club with which we are familiar, the Union League of Philadelphia, has a particularly progressive food and beverage programme with multiple dining outlets. They have even purchased an independent restaurant for use by its members when they are on holiday at the shore.

Yacht club members' perspective

Yacht clubs too offer food and beverage to their members, although there can be some minor differences in offerings and service. While many members who dine at their country club are just coming off the golf course, yacht clubs cater to members whose social lives revolve around their boats. As one club manager put it, "our members are grateful to be alive", meaning that they are high from the exhilaration of sailing.

While the expectations of yacht club members are similar, the bar is a more celebrated component of the clubhouse. Except for the larger yacht clubs, there may be fewer dining options within the clubhouse. However, yacht clubs offer some services that are not offered elsewhere. Some of these include food deliveries to member boats who are spending the day on the water, sailing.

Operational perspective

Except for the smallest of clubs, clubs (city, country, yacht, etc.) will offer a variety of dining options for their members - multiple spaces, multiple menus and a range of settings from casual to formal. For instance, golfers (or tennis players) coming off the golf course or tennis courts for a burger and a beer require one type of offering. Members entertaining clients for lunch require another. And members bringing their extended families to the club for a weekend differ require yet another. The various types of dining venues are discussed below.

Types of dining in clubs
Formal dining

As society becomes more casual, people in general (including club members) look more for casual dining experiences. Even though formal dining in clubs is less common that it once was, it still exists. In fact, some have referred to clubs as being the last bastion of fine dining. Many clubs still have a formal dining room or, at the very least, offer periodic formal dining occasions, for instance on weekend nights, or once a month. Formal dining often consists of a large, ornate dining room. In a city club, it is probably the most elegant space in the building, may have high ceilings and artwork on the walls. In a country club, it often has oversized windows, overlooks the golf course and has bright colors. In a yacht club, it would most certainly overlook the water.

In either type of club, fine dining denotes a high level of service, uniformed wait staff, well-appointed tables, white tablecloths, ample space between tables, comfortable chairs, is expensive and has high quality food and a robust wine list. They may also require proper attire, including ties and jackets for men.

Members may dine in the fine dining room for special occasions, when entertaining clients, for holiday celebrations and for a host of other reasons. It was a popular dining option for many years (and generations) as it showcased the best that a club had to offer and complemented the needs of a particular segment of society. And for those club members who wanted something less formal, there were usually more casual options – formal dining on one end of the spectrum, the bar/grill on the other end and a mixed grill in between.

That said, fine dining is changing. At one time, eating in the formal dining room required that members get dressed up and act in a certain way. Just like fine dining in restaurants has changed though, the demand for a more casual dining experience in clubs is also increasing as members get younger and norms change. Clubs have addressed this in one of several ways – by casualizing their formal dining rooms to make them more enticing; by retaining their formal dining rooms but scaling them down; by limiting the service times for fine dining and offering fine dining once a week or once a month; or eliminating it entirely. Only in the more traditional and established clubs does formal dining remain unchanged.

Over the last generation, society in general has become more casual. This change came late to clubs but is still impacting them significantly. As this is being written, clubs around the world are grappling with whether to relax their dress codes, whether to allow jeans, and whether to allow mobile (cell) phones on the property. One of the results of this trend, has impacted club dining and increased the interest and popularity of casual dining venues in clubs.

Casual dining

As fine dining has decreased in popularity, there has been a shift in demand towards more casual dining. This change has been occurring over the last 15 – 20 years. In previous generations, casual dining was defined as the counterpoint to formal dining. Over time, clubs have revamped their dining rooms, relaxed their dress codes, updated their dining options and generally made dining more family-friendly. All of these changes have served to make casual dining at clubs the most popular option. Casual dining rooms incorporate a relaxed feel with more casual service combined with moderately priced menu items. They tend to be more contemporary in design as well, since many of the rooms have been redesigned in the last decade or so.

James Rogers (of Rogers McCagg Architects and Interior Designers) shared his observations on the changes he has seen in club design over the last ten years. While dining spaces are indeed becoming more casual, according to Rogers, the biggest change in design has been the variety of seating choices available for diners. Not everybody likes to eat at a traditional 4-top, so spaces are being designed to be more flexible and more diverse. For instance, clubs are creating 'pub- like' atmospheres to appeal to a wider range of members.

As an example, Rogers mentions a project that his company did 15 years ago - they designed a grill room for a club in the northeastern USA. Previously, members would have a cocktail in the lounge, receive a menu and then order and move into dining room for their meal. Then, the new grill room was designed with a bar. At first, the club leaders did not think the bar would be used, but just a few short years later, these areas have become the center of activity. Rogers goes on to explain the popularity of the new space as being a result of diverse seating and seating arrangements (high tops, settees, banquets, booths, and conventional tables), community/club tables, and a bar that offers a place for 'gathering'. Together, the design and layout work to create a more inclusive environment for all from football fans to families. In short, dining spaces have evolved into spaces for socializing. When asked about other design changes, Rogers emphasized other elements of the servicescape: a lot of attention is being paid to acoustics and lighting. His company typically does not carpet bar areas but does carpet casual dining spaces. Also, lighting has to be adjustable so as to be more intimate and more finely adjustable.

Photo 6.2: The Harvard Club – bar and dining room. Courtesy of the Harvard Club of Boston

Finally, much of the dining/gathering/socializing in clubs is moving from the inside to the outside. Outdoor dining has always been popular at clubs, but is now becoming much more inviting with increased seating, increased comfort and the addition of outdoor firepits (which he suggests is included in every current project they are hired for). He summarized the changes that are taking place by saying that casual dining spaces are being designed to encourage socializing more than anything else.

There may also be food and beverage served in the locker rooms, for the convenience of members. In addition to food and beverage service (with table service) in the clubhouse, clubs may have 'satellite' operations throughout the operation, with more limited menus. Food and beverage may be provided on the golf course (the hallway house is usually at the 'turn') and; in various sports centers, such as the fitness centre. Also, some clubs have gone so far as to introduce food trucks, such as at Medinah Country Club in Illinois and Farmington Country Club in Virginia. The trend in clubs is give members what they want, where they want.

So, to summarize, casual dining has moved from simply providing a counterpoint to formal dining to becoming the most desirable and active spaces in the entire club. By casualizing these spaces, clubs have reinvigorated their entire food and beverage programs, while at the same time, not sacrificing revenues. It should also be added that casual dining in clubs have adopted many of the popular elements of fine dining – professional service, well executed menus, and robust wine lists.

Photo 6.3: Manchester Country Club. Courtesy of the Manchester Country Club.

Differentiating factors

A few other things must be said about à la carte dining before we move on to events and catering. These are key differentiating factors that future managers must bear in mind. These include food and beverage minimums, tipping, how members pay, and food and beverage metrics.

Food and beverage minimums

First, we must mention something called a food and beverage (or food) 'minimum'. This is a charge that members incur in addition to dues and fees for other services. The food minimum at clubs is the pre-defined minimum amount that members must pay each period (monthly or quarterly) for food in the dining outlets. The philosophy behind this is that it encourages members to use the restaurant more than they would otherwise. The downside is that some members resent it, however, it exists as a fixture in many clubs. According to ClubBenchmarking, the median food minimum (for their subscribing clubs) is $600 USD per year. Again, that means that members must spend a minimum of $600 on dining during the year. If they do not meet the minimum, they are charged the difference. There are members in every club who, for one reason or another, do not meet the minimum. The result is a fund titled 'unspent minimums' and can run into tens of thousands of dollars each year.

Two last items relating to food minimums must be mentioned. First, some clubs place restrictions on what counts towards the minimum. For instance, some clubs do not count alcoholic drinks, while others do not count take-away food. Second, some clubs are rethinking food minimums, feeling that they can be viewed as punitive. These clubs have adopted several options including: (1) a spending minimum where any purchases at the club count; (2) a separate fee entirely that is unassociated which may go toward a capital project; and (3) awarding points for spending, much the way that airlines and hotels do – this results in 'rewards' rather than 'penalties'.

In short, there continue to be mixed feelings regarding minimums and some clubs seem to be taking steps to reposition them.

Tipping

A second differentiating factor in an (à la carte) club food and beverage operations is the way in which front-of-the-house employees are compensated. In most commercial restaurants, at least in the USA, servers receive a small hourly wage and then make up the rest of their wages through tips from customers. In contrast, most clubs pay their servers a higher hourly wage and in addition, may prohibit tipping entirely. This may be for a number of reasons, not the least of which is that members are already paying a lot to be members and clubs do not want members to always be burdened with the added hassle/burden of tipping. This is not unlike the reasoning behind pricing at all-inclusive resorts – the cost of all amenities and extras is simply built into the overall price. Additionally, members are like everyone else in society – some are going to be 'good' tippers and some are going to be 'poor' tippers. By not allowing tipping, clubs are able to avoid the type of behaviour that can be evident in restaurants, where servers request to serve the good tippers and avoid, or give substandard service to, the bad tippers. By prohibiting tipping, everyone pays the same flat service charge and all members, in theory, are treated similarly.

Of course, the potential down side of not allowing tipping is that for those servers who are motivated by the prospect of a (higher) tip, no such motivation exists. The motivation must come from wanting to provide all members with the same excellent service, regardless of conditions. Michael Robinson, MCM, sums up some of the reasons that tipping is uncommon in clubs:

- It represents an additional expense to the dining member
- Tipping may curry favored member and employee status
- Tips may create service inequalities such as speed of service, portion size, special orders, preferred tables, seating of large parties, and even foodservice in forbidden areas of the club.

How members pay

Most clubs do not allow cash purchases. Instead, in most private clubs, members are billed monthly for food and beverage purchases and other club charges incurred in the preceding month. The bill is due and payable upon receipt and the terms are net 30. In most clubs, delinquency is not an option and members must be current to remain members in good standing at their club. On rare occasions, members can be suspended from using the club in the event that the indebtedness is not satisfied.

Food and beverage metrics/profitability

Successful food and beverage operations are those that meet sales and expense projections. Terms such as profitability and contribution to margin can be measured in terms of cost of goods sold (COGS) and total operating payroll (TOP). When you combine these items, you have prime cost. It is possible in the private club industry, because of a multitude of factors, to have prime costs of 104% of sales. This will be discussed in the finance chapter.

Other metrics that are used to measure performance in food and beverage operations is total sales, food cost percentage (COGS/sales), labour cost percentage (total labour cost/sales), average cheque (total sales/covers) and variance analysis (difference between forecasts and actual results).

Events - banquets and catering

Banquets and catering are big business in clubs, tend to be profitable, and can go a long way in subsidizing à la carte operations. The reasons they are profitable are numerous. When there is a combination of pricing, limited menus choices, fixed hours of event activity and attendance guarantees, there is the potential for profit.

More and more of our students are becoming interested in event management. Often, when students think of events, they think of hotels, restaurants and event management companies. We remind them that banquets and catering (or events) are a big part of club food and beverage operations. In some clubs, events are the driving force in the food and beverage department and provide much of the revenue and profits. Some of the most interesting, creative and fun events that we have seen have been at clubs.

Events can be divided into two primary categories: (1) member events and (2) nonmember events. *Member events* are events that are exclusively for members or members and their guests. These may include everything from small cocktail parties or birthday parties to weddings, regattas, and golf tournaments. Almost always, they include food and beverage.

Nonmember events are those that are provided for guests who are not members of the club. Most clubs require that these events be sponsored by a member. It is important to understand the distinction between member and nonmember events for the following reasons.

We make the distinction between these two types of events for three reasons. First, some clubs value their privacy so much that they may have a policy against hosting nonmember events. That is, the club is for members only. Members typically pay a lot of money for the privileges associated with membership and may resent it when parts of the club, or even the entire club, are unavailable to them because nonmembers may be using it.

Second, for those clubs that do allow nonmember events, they can be more profitable than member events. This is because clubs may charge room rentals, higher service charges, and higher menu prices than they do for member events. Indeed, this may be the primary reason that many clubs decide to allow nonmember events. They understand that the contribution to the bottom-line is more substantial.

Finally, there can be tax implications of hosting nonmember events. As we noted in Chapter 3, in the USA, the IRS only allows tax-exempt clubs from deriving a certain percentage of their gross revenues (15%) from nonmember sources. This obviously puts limits on how many and what types of nonmember events can be hosted. This rule is in place to discourage tax-exempt businesses from operating like a commercial establishment, while avoiding income taxes on nonmember business. We will return to the 15% rule in Chapter 9 when we look at club finances.

Types of events

Whether clubs host member events, nonmember events, or both, events represent an important part of the social and financial fabric of clubs. Events will often be managed separately from à la carte operations as well. In large and (typically) for-profit clubs, there may be a sales person, or even a sales team. There will also be a dedicated staff member who looks after the actual event. This will consist of a manager or supervisor, and dedicated banquet staff who may work on an on-call basis or on a part-time basis. Many of the part-timers may be local college or university students.

Events may take place in any number of rooms in the clubhouse and, indeed, some events are so large that they take over the entire clubhouse (such as a wedding). This is largely dependent on the layout and design of the clubhouse. Many newer clubhouses are being designed with this in mind, with large contiguous spaces that can be closed off with folding doors.

Other events may be held on the golf course, the docks, by the tennis courts, at the pool, in a private dining room, or under a canopy/tent. In fact, one club that we know of does not have any banquet space per se and hosts all of its events under a canopy/tent on the grounds, which stays up virtually all summer (which is their busy season).

A special type of nonmember event is known as an 'outing', which is defined as a group which spends the day at a club engaged in sports (usually golf) and a dining event, often including an awards ceremony. An outing is usually associated with a nonmember event, is typically golf related (in golf clubs) and the group participating in the outing may be a corporate group, a non-profit organization or a charity, among others. Outings are often held on a day when they will not interfere with regular operations (usually Monday) and can be very lucrative for the host club.

In an effort to expand their services to members, as well as to generate additional revenues, some clubs are offering more 'off premises' events. These may be held at members' homes (typically in a development club), or anywhere else that a member desires. Some clubs choose not to offer these, as they require additional expertise and equipment.

The last point we would like to make regarding events is their importance to the sustainability of a club. Events are often the first exposure that a nonmember might have to a club, so their experience has to be a positive one. This is also an important factor to keep in mind for clubs which may be debating the value of hosting events – that is, the prospect of recruiting new members.

Photo 6.4: Farmington Country Club Food Truck. Courtesy of Farmington Country Club (Virginia).

Bar and beverage service

So far, we have discussed à la carte dining (formal dining and casual dining) and events at clubs. These are the two primary food related areas. There is also the bar, so now let's turn our attention to bar and beverage service. This has always been an important component in clubs which are licensed to serve alcoholic beverages. Clubs which are licensed will typically offer spirits, beer and wine for their members. Spirits have always been popular and, if we can generalize, clubs members have always preferred premium spirits and have historically received what is referred to as a 'club pour' meaning a generous pour. But more and more, club members are developing preferences for boutique wines and craft beers. As a result, clubs must maintain not only a diverse range of beverages but also, a wide range.

The bar area at a club is often a focal point. In days past, they were often located in the Mens' Grill, which was off-limits to women. Times have changed though and bar areas have expanded (in their size and scope) and are becoming the social centres of clubs. This is occurring as bars become more inclusive, offer a broader range of beverages, and also offer a greater diversity of food.

We should also add that even with generous pours, the beverage side of the industry can be more profitable, at least on a percentage basis, While cost of food (as a percentage of sales) may range from 35 % to 45 %, the cost of beverages (as a percentage of sales) can be significantly lower.

Photo 6.5: Karachi Club Snack Bar. Courtesy of the Karachi Club.

Trends in food and beverage

Food and beverage in clubs is currently undergoing a mini-renaissance. Clubs are experimenting with new products, services and distribution channels (e.g. food trucks). And menus are getting more dynamic. It would be a challenge to pick up any club management publication today and not be able to find a feature article celebrating the food and beverage programme at one club or another.

One recent issue of *Club Management* magazine identified several clubs that are thinking, outside of the box. One club is brewing its own beer while another hosts a build-your-own pizza night. Others are going all out with local and organic ingredients. What clubs are finding is that members are becoming more receptive to innovative ideas in this area. Every club that we know is stepping up their food and beverage offerings. Other food and beverage trends are explored more fully in Chapter 10.

Challenges moving forward

While we have presented food and beverage as an exciting, innovative, and potentially profitable area, challenges remain. Clubs continue to be at a disadvantage, when compared to commercial restaurants. They are serving a limited population with certain constraints that commercial restaurants do not have.

Their costs can be higher because of their size in both food and labour. They may also have several operational inefficiencies (mostly due to aging infrastructures) that boards of directors might be reluctant to address. In many markets, they are experiencing increasing competition – for guests and for labour. We hear from many managers that they are experiencing labour shortages, especially in the back-of-the-house. And, finally, they are faced with the ongoing challenge of keeping members happy by balancing traditional menu items with those that are new and exciting. Despite the challenges though, club food and beverage has gained a certain respectability (and pride) among members.

A slightly opinionated conclusion

Charles Dickens wrote: "It was the best of times, it was the worst of times", in *A Tale of Two Cities* (1859). For many clubs and many club managers, the food and beverage operation can be a mixed blessing. For some members, food and beverage is their reason for belonging. For others, food and beverage is a necessary amenity. The most successful club managers are able to balance food and beverage wants and needs for the vast majority of members by providing a quality club experience for each member visit. We continue to hear from managers that board members want to know why they aren't able to make money. They may hear it in different forms:

"Why doesn't our food and beverage program make money?"

"Why don't we run our food and beverage program like a restaurant?"

"The restaurant down the street makes money, why doesn't our club?"

These are some of the questions we often hear and that club managers are faced with every day. Often the people asking the questions are board members or others, who are sincerely questioning the value and purpose of food and beverage in a club, without a complete understanding of it. For us, the question is: *"Is a club food and beverage programme an amenity or a profit center?"* Once a club decides that it is an amenity to be offered to members, with certain built-in costs, there is comfort in knowing that its viability is largely dependent upon subsidies from the flow of dues. That said, some clubs (particularly nonequity clubs) are able to make money by tailoring the menu, limiting hours and watching costs. Companies such as ClubBenchmarking, are helping club managers educate their boards about the real constraints that food and beverage departments face.

Discussion questions

1　Identify all of the factors that you think make the management of a food and beverage operation in a club different from a commercial restaurant operation.

2　Discuss some of the recent innovations that you have observed in club food and beverage operations.

3　What do you think would be some of the more challenging aspects of managing food and beverage in clubs?

References

Barrows, C.W. (1997). Food and beverage operations in clubs. In J. Perdue (Ed.). *Contemporary Club Management* (pp. 303 – 334), AH&LA: Lansing, MI.

Larsen, R, (2017). What's working in F & B now, *Club Management*, July/August.

7 Recreation

Introduction

One of the things that makes a club into a club is that it brings together people with a common interest. Sometimes the common interest is food and beverage, but often it is a recreational activity, of which the most prominent is golf. But there are many other recreational activities that take place at clubs and this chapter will discuss many (though not all) of them. Club activities are many and varied. It is important for students to understand the individual activities, and particularly: (1) who participates; (2) how they are managed; (3) how they interact with other activities/areas of the club; (4) whether they are cost centres or profit centres; and (5) trends and changes affecting these activities and their popularity.

Golf

Let's begin with one of the longest lived, most celebrated sports and one which has an incredibly rich history. Golf is perhaps the most popular sport at clubs (and is primarily offered at golf clubs and country clubs). It has been played at clubs in Scotland since the 1600s, expanded to England, was later exported to clubs in other Commonwealth countries, as well as the USA, and continues to be popular. To nonplayers, the game of golf is surrounded by a mystique - in addition to its long history, it has had numerous famous players (many of whom are known only by their first names or nicknames such as Tiger, The Golden Bear, and The Shark), and is associated with grand golf courses such as St. Andrews, Pebble Beach, Augusta National, Royal Melbourne Golf Club, etc. It is a truly international game. Exhibit 7.1 profiles golf in Australia.

Golf is a game with its own historic archives, a hall of fame, and its own television channel! It is also a very challenging game to play. Most players who want to learn to play it, take lessons. It is not the sort of sport that one learns how to play in one's backyard or in the neighbourhood playground. For all of these reasons, it is perceived in a certain light. But let's start with the basics of the game.

Exhibit 7.1: Golf in Australia

Golf is a prominent sport in Australia, having been played there since the 1830s. Some of the oldest clubs in the world were established there. According to *Golf Australia*, there are over 1,300 golf clubs in the country (mostly clustered in New South Wales) and there were an estimated 500,000 players in the late 1990s, when golf participation peaked. Since its peak, however, the number of clubs (and members) has declined, although the number of rounds overall, has increased over the last year. The golf industry in Australia, as elsewhere, is trying to raise the visibility of the game as well as to introduce it to under-represented groups. Several golf-related initiatives have been introduced in recent years including MyGolf (a national junior programme), Swing Fit (for women) and Inclusion (for disabled golfers).

The information in this profile was compiled from the Golf Australia web site (www. golf.org.au) whose mission is to "… raise the level of interest and participation in the game from grassroots golfers through to the elite levels, spectators, volunteers and associated industry bodies."

The game of golf

Golf is played on either a 9 hole or 18 hole course (although some courses may have 27 or even 36 holes), where a player begins on the 'tee' and ends on the 'green', with the fairway, rough, bunkers (hazards), and perhaps water, in between.

It is generally played (and scored) on an individual basis although it is common to play as part of a foursome. Each hole has a 'par', that is the number of strokes that it should take a player to reach the green (and sink the ball) from the tee. This is based on the expectation that a golfer will require two putts per hole. For instance, a par 4 would include two putts, as would a par 5, etc.

Bear Right: This dogleg-right par 4 plays from elevated tees to a large landing area. Aim just to the left of the fairway bunkers; long hitters can carry them. Watch for the hidden pond on the left. The moderately uphill, short-iron second shot is to a green with a severe false front.

YARDS
■ 366
■ 335
□ 301
▨ 276

Figure 7.1: Hole 3, from a guide to the course at Lake Winnipesaukee Golf Club

Pars are also established for 9 hole courses and 18 hole courses, which equal the sum of the individual pars of the holes. In its simplest form, the player with the fewest strokes to play the course is the winner, although 'handicaps' are often taken into consideration and there are many different variations on the basic format. Penalties are also invoked under certain situations (which result in the addition of a stroke or strokes to the score).

While every golf course is different, there are several major categories of courses including *parkland* (manicured, lots of trees), *links* (near the coast, fewer trees, grasses), and *desert* courses (as might be found in the American West or the Middle East). The people who design these courses are known as golf course designers or architects and there are several of whom are well known including Donald Ross, Robert Trent Jones, A.W. Tillinghast, and Stanley Thompson. Architects are, rightly, strongly associated with the courses they design. For example, one might hear reference to a 'Donald Ross course'. Donald Ross (1872 – 1948) was born in Scotland, emigrated to the USA and designed courses in the USA, Canada and Cuba. As with other architects, he had certain signature features and designs, for which he is still known. More recently, former professional golfers such as Bobby Jones, Jack Nicklaus and Arnold Palmer have also designed and developed courses. Often when contemporary architects design a course, it is in conjunction with a full-scale development with a club and includes a real estate component.

Developing a golf course is an expensive undertaking. A typical 18 hole course can require 60 hectares (or about 150 acres) of land and cost a lot of money to build. In *Building A Practical Golf Facility,* by Michael Hurdzan of the American Society of Golf Course Architects, examples of actual courses range from about $800,000 USD to over $10 million USD. Factors affecting the total cost include the amount and cost of land, who designs it, and its features.

To understand golf, it is important to know that the golf profession and the rules of golf are overseen by different entities. The United States Golf Association (USGA) and the Royal and Ancient (R & A) oversee the rules of golf, which are updated periodically. There are only 34 major rules in the game but the most recent rulebook runs to 121 pages and does not include decisions (official rulings) or etiquette. Please note that, as we write, the USGA and R & A are proposing major rules changes, to be implemented in 2019. The rules are aimed at a major simplification and update. Information about the new rules can be found at: www.usga.org/content/usga/home-page/rules-hub/rules-modernization/text/golfs-new-rules-faqs.html

In conjunction, the Professional Golfers Association of America (and affiliated associations) exists to "establish and elevate the standards of the profession and to grow interest and participation in the game of golf." Among other things, the PGA of America (and others) promote the game of golf, offer professional development for PGA professionals, and oversee the credentialing of its members. PGA America should not be confused with PGA TOUR, which manages professional tournaments such as the AT&T Pebble Beach Pro-Am, FedExCup, and 130 other tournaments.

Now, before we go on, students should know that one does not have to play golf in order to manage a golf or country club, but they should know the rules and should have an appreciation for the game so that they can discuss it with their golf playing members. We have known many managers of clubs who did not play golf (or play much) and who were successful managers. On the other hand, a manager who does not play nor show an interest in the game would probably have challenges advancing their career. It is also important for students (as future managers) to understand the game because of the extent of interaction that they will have with the Director of Golf and Golf Course Superintendent (discussed below).

Who participates?

The game of golf has been stereotyped to such a degree that many of us would be led to believe that it is the bastion of middle-aged white men. While this was probably close to the truth at one time, the game is now played by an increasingly diverse group with respect to age, gender and race. However, one cannot overlook certain factors such as cost and access that might limit a person's ability to enjoy the game and limit access to certain groups. That said, the PGA as well as other groups are trying to increase the visibility of the game as well as access to it. One group, First Tee, has as its mission to provide golf education to young people and, in addition, offers programs to reduce the cost of playing.

In clubs, the answer to this question is a little different. As we have learned, clubs are comprised of members with different club privileges. In a country (or golf) club, the members who play are typically those who have full or equity memberships (or golf memberships) which carry with it the highest entrance fees, the highest dues, voting rights and the greatest use of the facility. Members in other membership categories usually have reduced playing privileges, or perhaps no golf privileges at all. For instance, a social member would typically have full run of the clubhouse but might be limited to four (or so) rounds of golf per year (a round is defined as the number of holes that a member plays whether it is 1, 9, or 36). Other members might be allowed to play but their tee times (when they are able to play) might not be as favourable. Full dues paying members as described above would be allowed to play 'for free' (covered by their dues) but might incur extra expenses for use of a caddy, a golf cart, or to bring a guest. So, for clubs which offer golf, it represents a primary reason for joining the club and for paying associated dues and additional costs.

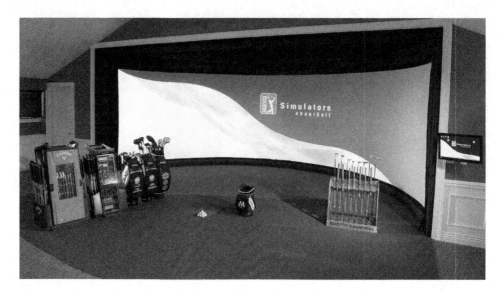

Photo 7.1: A display of equipment, Manchester Country Club

Operations

In clubs, golf appears to operate as two (almost separate) departments with different but converging responsibilities. The first area, or department, is called simply the Greens Department (run by the Golf Course Superintendent). This department looks after the care and maintenance of the golf course which includes mowing, irrigation, repairs, seeding, thatching, application of pesticides and insecticides, trimming of trees and anything else that affects the physical play of the course. This department would also look after any longer term improvements or upgrades such as course reconstruction or improvements to the irrigation system.

The second department may simply be known as the Golf Department and is overseen by a golf professional or director of golf. The director of golf would oversee the entire 'playing' (or operations) side of the game which would include: (1) management of play; (2) lessons; (3) the 'golf pro' shop (where merchandise is sold); (4) tournaments; and (5) Staffing. With regard to this last category, the director of golf would oversee additional golf professionals, staff in the pro shop, tournament staff, caddies, starters, marshals, and anyone else associated with the playing of the game. The director of golf and the superintendent (and general manager) would be in almost constant communication about the condition of the course, possible restrictions on play and areas of the course needing attention.

Photo 7.2: Golf Pro shop at Manchester Country Club

In member-owned clubs, the Green (or Greens) Committee works with the superintendent to ensure that the condition and playability of the course is what it should be. In addition, the Golf Committee (or Golf Activities Committee) works with the director of golf to ensure that all of the golf programmes that are available meet the needs of its members. In both cases, the committees are composed of members who are interested in the sustainability of the game of golf and its course, at the club.

Because the game requires such a large investment and has such a large member participation rate (proportionately), it demands a lot of attention. According to the most recent PKF Clubs in Town and Country, the average club (with golf) can count on an average of 52% of their revenue to be generated by dues and an additional 13% of revenue to be generated by golf associated fees. This means that almost two-thirds of overall revenues are generated directly or indirectly by golf playing members. On the expense side, however, golf courses require a tremendous amount of care and upkeep, representing a proportionately large expense for clubs. In addition to daily attention to the course, golf courses need to be periodically upgraded which can cost into the hundreds of thousands of dollars. Upgrades may include the redesign of parts of the course, repairs to the irrigation system, cutting and trimming of trees, etc. Such upgrades are typically paid for in one of four ways: from the operational budget, capital reserves, assessment of members and/or debt (in the way of loans).

Tournaments

Club members have a variety of opportunities to play golf at their clubs. They may go out on a whim on a weekend morning, assuming an available 'tee time'; they might play as part of a regular foursome; they might be part of a league which would typically play at a regular time each week; or they may participate in tournaments. Golf tournaments, which can be limited to members or might include nonmembers, are a focal point of the golf programme at clubs. They involve a great deal of planning and communication among the general manager, director of golf, superintendent, and the committees, as well as other departments. In short, they showcase the club, its members, and the game of golf. Tournaments can run the gamut from those that are limited to golf playing members to international tournaments that a club may choose to host (such as any of the major LPGA or PGA tournaments). In addition to engaging members, tournaments may also bring additional revenue and prestige to a club. A significant portion of staff time is devoted to the planning and managing of tournaments. Tournaments can last for just a few hours to several days, for instance over a holiday weekend. They are an effective means of engaging members, promoting the game, showcasing the club and, in some cases, generating revenue. One of the fixtures in tournament play at clubs is the 'member/guest tournament', which can take place throughout the golf season. It allows members to bring their guests (and team up with them). It usually involves at least one day of play, and an awards banquet. Member/Guest tournaments are effective ways of keeping members engaged, proud of their club, and provides the prospect of attracting new members.

Summary

Golf has been a popular game for hundreds of years now, with some ebbs and flows over the years. Students might have heard reference to the 'Tiger Effect' which alludes to the rise (and subsequent fall and rise again) of Tiger Woods, and everything that he did to increase the popularity of golf and tournament play, particularly among underrepresented groups.

That said, there are questions about the state of the golf industry and the popularity of the game in today's society where there are so many other options. Golf would seem to fly in the face of some societal trends given its time demands, expense and, in some cases, advance planning required. A game can take four or more hours to play which can be a hardship for those with families, young children, or with other demands on their time.

In general, golf participation is down since its peak (in several countries), although there is evidence that it is starting to rebound. However, please note two things. First, participation is generally measured in 'rounds', where a round represents a game played by a single golfer where the game may be 1, 9, 18 or X number of holes. Second, golf is not only played at private clubs but also at public (or daily fee) courses, resorts and municipal courses. Daily fee courses offer golfers a less expensive alternative to joining (and playing at) a club. So private clubs are faced with competition from daily fee courses as well as from other activities which may require less skill, less time, and less of a financial commitment. Anecdotally, as the cost of a round decreases to $40 USD, participation increases.

Clubs (and the broader golf industry) have adopted several strategies to try to combat the challenges they are facing. First, they are trying to introduce kids to the game at younger and younger ages, through camps, clinics and the like. Second, they are introducing variations on the game – millennials may be familiar with Topgolf, foot golf and Frisbee golf. Clubs are also investing in golf simulators where golfers can 'play' golf, much like a video game. Finally, more clubs are experimenting with three (or six) hole loops, which cut down on the time requirement and, in some cases, developing courses with 3 par holes (as opposed to 4 or more).

In the end, golf courses are expensive to build and maintain in an environment of changing attitudes toward the game. Add to this the over-supply of courses (both public and private) in certain regions, and some clubs have had to make the hard decision to close, sell or convert to semi-private or daily fee. This is particularly true in North America. However, it is important to remember that golf is still a popular sport and that many clubs still have a vibrant golf programme. One example of a club where golf is thriving is at the Winchester Country Club, outside of Boston. In addition to their 18 hole course, they have recently added a virtual golf area, a Learning Centre (complete with multi-camera video capabilities), and a new 'Wee Course', which is a 6 hole course for use by junior golfers, for teaching, and for golfers who opt for shorter option. Golf will be discussed further in Chapter 10.

Racquet sports

Racquet (or racket) sports are also very popular in private clubs. For instance, country clubs may offer tennis and/or other racquet sports. City clubs often offer squash, racquetball and badminton. Racquet clubs (offering exclusively racquet sports) exist, tennis clubs being the most popular; and even badminton clubs exist in some countries (for instance the Badminton and Racquet Club in Toronto offers it as a primary activity). Racquet sports can include a wide variety of activities – the only thing having in common is the use of a racquet. Some of the more traditional, and common, racquet sports would include tennis, paddle tennis, badminton, squash, racquet ball, and, increasingly, pickle ball.

Rather than discussing each and all of these sports, we will focus on tennis which, despite the increasing popularity of other sports, continues to be one of the most popular. Growth in tennis, like golf, has been flat in recent years with certain demographic groups playing less than in previous generations. According to one general manager, adults who took up the game in the 1980s (and 1990s) are still playing and younger players are still taking it up but it is losing market share to other racquet sports and other activities. That said, tennis has many of the elements that all age groups might find attractive, including the fact that it is a skill based activity, requires less time than certain other sports, is relatively affordable, and is a good aerobic workout. It also attracts both men and women.

The Wightman Tennis Center (in Massachusetts) is an excellent example of a club that was largely established by and for tennis players, and currently offers extensive programming on its 16 courts. However, it is not just limited to tennis and, offers indoor and outdoor pools and extensive fitness facilities. It is an active club with many options for its members.

Kurt Douty, general manager of the Wightman Tennis Center, shared with us that his club offers a wide variety of tennis programming for all age groups, including for children as young as four. Younger players are accommodated with lower nets, lighter balls and smaller courts. Mr. Douty states that his members enjoy many aspects of the game and that some players are attracted by its social nature and others for the competition. Still others enjoy the fitness component.

Unlike golf, where the dimensions of the course are left to the creativity of the designer, tennis is played on a standardized court which measures 78 feet long by 27 feet (for singles) or 36 feet (for doubles) with a 3 foot net down the middle. It may be played by two players (singles) or four players (doubles).

Players use a racquet whose surface is strung and must conform to the International Tennis Federation (ITF) rules, a portion of which reads:

"The racket shall not exceed 73.7 cm (29.0 inches) in overall length, and 31.7 cm (12.5 inches) in overall width. The hitting surface shall not exceed 39.4 cm (15.5 inches) in overall length, when measured parallel to the longitudinal axis of the handle, and 29.2 cm (11.5 inches) in overall width, when measured perpendicular to the longitudinal axis of the handle."

The composition of the racquet, the diameter and the weight keep evolving as stronger and lighter materials, such as kevlar, are introduced. The biggest change to racquets over the last 20 years has been the introduction of polyester strings. This allows for much more spin on the ball. Tennis equipment has changed, much the same way that other sports equipment has, including golf clubs (and skis, and snowboards, and bicycles, and boats, etc.).

And, of course, the racquet is used to hit a ball, which must also conform to ITF specifications. Balls must also be of uniform size, can be pressurized or not, are covered in fabric, and come in different specifications depending on the desired speed of play, playing surface and altitude.

One player (or team) serves the ball to the receiving team and serves until they lose a point. Points are scored on every serve and the first player or team to score four points wins the game (but must win by two points). Games are played as part of a set (which consists of six games but where the winning team must win by two games; for instance 6 – 4). At 6-6 players play a tie-breaker, which follows specific criteria. A match consists of the best of three (or five) sets. At the professional level all matches are best of 3 sets, with the exception of the 4 Grand Slam tournaments, where the men play best of 5 sets.

Courts are made from a variety of materials – traditionally they were made of grass (lawn) but now the four main surfaces that they are made from include grass, clay, hard surface and carpet. They each have their advantages and disadvantages which include speed of play, cost to build and maintain, and risk of injury. Again, and similar to golf courses, tennis courts require continuous upkeep, no matter the structural makeup. They require daily maintenance, seasonal attention, and, periodically, must be resurfaced and even replaced.

Tennis courts, regardless of the surface, may also be lit (allowing members to play at night) and/or covered (allowing members to play year-round). While both of these features enhance the tennis experience, they also increase the cost of operation and maintenance.

The International Tennis Federation (ITF) governs the game on a global basis including: administration and regulation; organizing international tournaments, structuring the game; developing the game; and promoting the game (ITF, 2018). Different associations in different countries oversee the credentialing/certification of tennis professionals (it is the USTA in the USA, Tennis Australia in Australia, etc.).

Tennis, at the club level, is managed by the director of tennis, or the tennis professional, who typically has multiple years of experience, certification as a player and as a teacher. The director of tennis has a wide range of responsibilities including programming, staffing, giving lessons, managing court times, managing tournaments, budgeting and looking after the tennis (pro) shop. They may have one or more assistants, depending upon the size of the club, to help in the tennis shop, stringing, give lessons, and/or manage tournaments and leagues. As other racquet sports gain popularity, the director of tennis is expanded at some clubs to include oversight of other sports. At some clubs, the director of tennis may be a contractual position (independent contractors are discussed in Chapter 4), for the same reason some golf professionals are.

The director of tennis (and his or her staff) is supported, in member-owned clubs, by tennis committees. The Tennis Committee operates much as the Golf Committee would – serving at the behest of the Board of Directors and making recommendations regarding the state of the facility and programming. Tennis committees are composed of playing members who help advise with regard to programming, rates, budgets, policies, contracts and tournaments. In smaller clubs, there will usually be a single tennis committee while in larger clubs there may be several with more narrowly defined roles.

Who plays?

Much of the activity with tennis membership is with members playing against other members. This often takes place in the way of 'ladders', round-robins, and other types of intra-club or intra-league competitions. There may also be leagues where members play against members from other clubs, and more traditional tournaments, with wider participation. Some of the leagues are sanctioned by different tennis authorities, such as the USTA, or regional authorities.

In addition, most clubs have programs for juniors, including camps, clinics, etc. This is especially true at clubs that are trying to build a sustainable tennis program. One manager of a club in New Hampshire, who sees tennis participation at his club contracting, offers a variety of programs for younger children, beginning at the age of 5. He has observed that when children reach their teens, they find other activities and distractions that take them away from tennis. Tennis at his club is an 'asset for families', although interest among older members is declining. He sees far less participation among adults than he did in the 1990s. According to the Tennis Industry Association (TIA), growth in tennis participation is slight, with most of the growth occurring in youth tennis, while the highest level of participation is with players between 25 and 34.

Tennis may be handled differently than golf within clubs. Typically, in a country club setting, there are fewer tennis players than there are golfers. Certainly full members at a country club will have tennis privileges. Social members may also be able to play at some clubs. However, some clubs may even have a tennis membership category, which would allow members to pay less in dues and to play tennis but would not allow them the same extensive privileges as a full member. For clubs that are trying to build their tennis programs, having a dedicated membership category for tennis players could help.

All of these programmes offer members opportunities to play throughout the day, season and year. For clubs that offer a variety of other activities, they will need to be aware of the possible 'cannibalization' effect. However, for clubs that want to cultivate the game amongst serious players, a strong program with opportunities for competition will be needed.

Trends

As with many other sports and activities, changes are taking place in tennis as new demographic groups take it up and as clubs look for new ways to engage their members. Tennis trends seem to be capitalizing on its already social and active attributes. One current trend is cardio tennis. According to Cardiotennis.com, "Cardio Tennis is a new, fun, group activity featuring drills to give players of all abilities an ultimate, high-energy workout." Kurt Douty, of the Wightman Tennis Center, describes it as being "an aerobics class held on a tennis court." In short cardio tennis combines music, movement and hitting tennis balls, for a full aerobic workout. Clubs have found that it is an effective way of capitalizing on the social aspects of tennis with members' needs for staying fit. It may also be fee-based, which can enhance club revenues. POP Tennis is another variation on tennis. It is similar to tennis but played on smaller courts, using shorter racquets and low pressure balls. Clubs are also incorporating greater uses of technology into their tennis programmes, developing 'smart courts' which can video players to use as a teaching method.

In addition, clubs continue to try to increase engagement through various means, including hosting exhibitions, often showcasing professional, or former professional, players. They are also combining tennis matches with social events.

Finally, tennis participation is being affected by the growing popularity of other racquet sports such as pickleball, paddle tennis, and indoor racquet sports. Some club members play multiple racquet sports, governed by their season, while others show preference for one over the others.

While tennis is not growing like it once did, it remains a popular sport which members can continue to play late into their lives. Advocates of the game point to its social and aerobic aspects, both of which bode well for its sustainability in clubs where both of these factors are valued.

Aquatics

Over the years, we have heard many club managers expound upon the challenges of managing a pool operation – from the food and beverage snack bar to the hiring of life guards to the safety issues. In fact, an old adage in the club goes something like this: the opening of the pool begins the 100 day war (referring to the typical season length). However, it seems that if a single club amenity can exemplify everything that represents how clubs are changing, it is the area of aquatics. As a result, managers' views of pools, and the role that they play in the club environment, seem to be changing as well. As we will see, a strong aquatics programme can enhance the membership experience and help a club cater more effectively to families, which is a primary objective for many clubs.

Similar to racquet sports, aquatics (swimming, etc.) are offered in a variety of club environments. Many country clubs have pools as do city and athletic clubs. Some clubs offer only aquatics (e.g. swimming clubs). And for some clubs it may be a central feature, for example clubs that are located on a lake or the sea (such as beach clubs).

As a club activity, it is similar to both golf and tennis (previously discussed) in that it requires a core group of members who are interested in supporting it. Like other sports too, clubs with strong aquatics programmes offer activities for juniors (under 16) as well as adults. As we will see, different groups have different needs.

Country clubs, and others, may have anything and everything from a single modest pool to an entire complex catering to a range of activities. Some even have complete pool developments that closely resemble water parks. Some clubs are developing mixed recreational facilities and using their pools as a central focus.

For instance, the Winchester Country Club has recently added a basketball court, ping pong, and a small playground to the recreation area adjacent to the pool. Another example is Fiddler's Elbow Country Club (in New Jersey, near New York City) which offers members a video game room, ping pong and bocce, all in the pool area.

Photo 7.3: Farmington Country Club Pool, courtesy of Farmington Country Club, Virginia.

Aquatics programming can be among the most multi-faceted activities in the club environment. Typically, clubs will offer various types of programmes for different ages and skill levels. For young children, the focus is usually on swimming (and diving) lessons. Lessons will typically progress with skill, from beginner to intermediate to advanced. For older children, the focus may be on endurance and technique. Also, at a certain age (young teenagers), may become interested in swimming competitively, so clubs may have a swim team which competes against other groups or clubs. One manager told us that kids then tend to 'age-out' sometime between 14 and 16 when they are presented with other ways to spend their time. Indeed, we have had several managers tell us that aquatics tend to be 'age dynamic', where interest levels ebb and flow in correlation to one's age.

For adults, there may be certain pool times reserved where they can swim laps or even compete, for health and wellness purposes. Other adults may use the pool as a way to rehab from injuries or to cross-train. Still others may participate in water aerobics programmes, which are becoming one of the most popular water activities. For instance, the Karachi Club (in Pakistan) offers a variety of programming including coaching sessions, water aerobics, and separate pool times for men and women.

In addition to formal lessons and competitions, clubs offer programmes that are more recreational in nature. This may involve water polo, and similar-water based activities. It all begins with the facility though. Some clubs are moving toward creating a water park environment. According to Rick Snellenger of Chambers, "To distinguish their pool facilities from others in the region, many private clubs are beginning to cite water parks as inspiration for their pool designs. Recreational elements not only give your pool facilities more entertainment value, but also increase perceived value among the membership and the 'return on experience', which is increasingly important in private clubs today" (http://clubviewblog. com/private-club-pools-create-membership-value/). With increased diversity of facilities, clubs are able to offer many options with the types of facilities, including: lap pools, kids' pool, and even indoor and outdoor options, depending upon the climate.

According to one manager, members want a resort environment, complete with options, amenities, extensive food and beverage, and poolside service. One example of a club that has taken their food and beverage services to another level is the Fiddler's Elbow Country Club. They have over 500 seats at the pool, and additional seating at the bar, as well as two cabanas. They have a separate pool menu, which includes extensive gluten free items, as well as acai bowls, sushi, and kabobs. Diners can even order off the dining room menu if they choose. In addition to the food options, the club has a full bar with its own beer and gin.

Finally, we should add that an inviting pool, combined with other recreational activities as well as food (and beverages) become a desired location for parties, special occasions, and simply socializing. The H. Chambers Company, which offers consulting services to clubs, has worked on many recent club pool projects. In a recent blog, they highlight five areas of a pool operation that can enhance value for members: adding interactive splash pads; upgrading the pool deck; improving the snack bar; having creative programing; and creating a social environment. (http://clubviewblog.com/poolside-necessities/).

Staffing

To support all of these activities, clubs must have adequate staffing support. In fact, the seasonal staffing at a club for aquatics can be quite extensive. Pool operations are general overseen by a pool manager (or pool director or swim director), who would have several direct reports including: assistant swim directors, activities directors, coaches and lifeguards (discussed below). The entire team works together to offer programmes for the members in a safe environment. One enterprising manager, who stressed the importance of having a good pool director, hires the swim coach from a local university. The coach works at the university for eight months and then takes over the pool operation at the club during the summer season.

At member-owned clubs, the members are also very involved with pool operations. Most clubs will have an Aquatics (or Pool) Committee which works in much the same way as golf and tennis committees do – by advising on programing, facilities, budgets and staffing. They play an important role in being additional 'eyes and ears' to an important area.

Safety and maintenance

Two other issues must be mentioned with regard to aquatics, and specifically, pools at clubs: safety and maintenance.

Pools require constant upkeep, both on a daily and on a long-term basis. Pools must be monitored regularly for pH levels, filtration and bacteria. Large clubs have staff members who can do this – others contract out this service. Either way, pool maintenance cannot be overlooked. pH levels are important because if they are not within an acceptable range, the water can irritate swimmers, interact negatively with chemicals in the pool and even damage the pool. Filtration removes dirt and debris. Sanitation is concerned with the bacteria levels in the pool. Most pools are treated with chlorine, bromine or saline. They all work to reduce the risk of illness that can result from a large number of people swimming together in a confined area.

Finally, a topic that is of ongoing concern for club managers is that of safety. Pools offer lots of opportunities for accidents, including injuries and even deaths. Clubs are not immune to these risks and take every opportunity to prevent them. Prevention involves safety protocols included in the design of the pool; having a set of standard operating procedures (SOPs); adequate staffing of lifeguards; threat assessments; and ongoing training. Rather than review every one of these, we will focus here on the importance of having properly trained lifeguards.

Clubs must hire (and staff) an adequate number of lifeguards. Lifeguards must be properly credentialed and should be subsequently trained by the clubs. A proper credential should serve as a threshold criteria for hiring. Lifeguard certifications are provided by many groups throughout the world including the YMCA, Red Cross, Royal Life Saving, Lifeguarding Services Australia, National Lifeguard, and several others. Certifications should indicate that the applicant has been trained in basic lifeguard skills, in-water rescue, basic first-aid, CPR, etc. A review of the Red Cross Lifeguarding manual is over 400 pages long, which is one indication how much a lifeguard needs to know. Clubs should not underestimate the need for qualifications and should plan to conduct training above and beyond what is provided with basic certifications.

Gerald Dworkin, of Lifesaving Resources, says that while lifeguards are the ones who are responsible for the safety and security of swimmers, clubs much be vigilant by doing threat assessments, conducting site-specific training, and planning and training for water based incidents. Gerald's company conducts water safety training for clubs. In all of his courses, he emphasizes prevention, recognition and active management.

Clubs must also be aware of new laws and regulations governing pools. One example of a relatively recent enactment in the USA is the Virginia Graeme Baker Pool and Spa Safety Act, which was passed in response to a drowning of a child, which was caused by the suction of the drainage system. As a result, the Act governs the sale and manufacture (and use) of what are known as Safety Vacuum Release Systems. Other laws govern pool design, enclosures, drainage and filtration systems and availability of safety equipment. Finally, pools are also regulated by accessibility laws, which require operators to remove barriers that might prevent swimmers with disabilities from access to the pool.

Fitness

Fitness facilities are one of the greatest growth areas in clubs of all kinds. Fitness facilities, as separate from the activities we have discussed earlier, combine strength training (weights and machines), cardio, instruction, training, classes and much more. Some clubs are incorporating fitness into broader health and wellness programmes which might include a spa, massage and personalized medical services.

We generally hear one of two things from club managers regarding fitness centres: (1) their club is currently considering adding a fitness facility; or (2) their club is planning to expand their fitness facility, because of unanticipated demand. Such is the demand for fitness in clubs. The popularity of fitness, like other activities we have discussed, in large part tracks age and demographic changes, but also cuts across various groups. And fitness trends in the broader society are generally being mirrored by fitness facilities and programmes in clubs. A large part of society is focusing on health and wellness, from their diets to exercise to stress reduction to their overall lifestyles. Clubs are able to capitalize on this and provide their members with services that support their lifestyles. While some clubs, such as the Karachi Club, have been focused on fitness for a very long time others have just begun to introduce it over the last 10 to 20 years. Those that have added it in recent years have done so for two reasons. First, their members have asked for it and, second, it is a way to keep their members on-site. Many managers have mentioned certain members of their club who typically spend a large part of the day playing golf, tennis, etc., only to have to go elsewhere to get their workout. This means that many members have had to join a second club (or gym) for their fitness regimen. Managers recognized this and began to find the time, money and space to introduce state-of-the-art facilities.

Photo 7.4: Fitness facility. Courtesy of Winchester Country Club (US)

One club in North Carolina invested heavily in a new fitness facility. According to a recent article in *Club and Resort Business*:

> *"Forsyth Country Club in Winston-Salem, N.C., completed a $5.2 million, 18,000-sq. ft. wellness and fitness center in September 2015, which Fitness Director Jenifer Johnson saw as an opportunity to also expand the club's fitness appeal. "As we saw the facility expand, we wanted to put into place something that's accessible to everybody—not just those who are already active, but also beginners and seniors," Johnson says.*
>
> *The facilities include three studios on the lower level: a 600-sq. ft. indoor cycle room with 20 Keiser bikes, featuring a well-lit stage for the instructor with blue streaming lights throughout the otherwise dark room, and surround sound ... ; a 700-sq. ft. yoga room with a hardwood floor, white wall sconces and fans, a view of the golf course and what Johnson calls an "overall zen quality"; the 1,200-sq. ft. general group exercise room, with 'loud' blue Mondo flooring to withstand heavy kettlebells and boot-camp exercises."* (https://clubandresortbusiness.com/2016/07/all-together-now/)

The example above effectively illustrates how a well-planned facility will attract different demographic groups, engage members and increase social interaction. Other clubs have found similar results.

Like other club activities though, a comprehensive fitness programme needs planning, support, and a long range vision. The best operations invest heavily in the physical facility. Several managers have said this strategy is based on the "build it and they will come" premise. These clubs have found that even when they have encountered resistance to the idea, the outcome has been successful.

In addition to the facility, which should include weights, machines, cardio equipment and space for classes, clubs should also have adequate staffing. This begins with a qualified Director of Fitness who will oversee the entire facility and staff. As with other sports and activities, having strong programming with good instructors is paramount. A trend in society (and in clubs) is to offer extensive classes which might include aerobics, Pilates, Zumba, spinning, yoga, and even martial arts. Members are also asking more and more for specialized programs like boot camp and other high intensity classes. Such classes, according to some club managers, are becoming increasingly popular with women. Clubs should hire qualified instructors for all of these activities, usually as independent contractors. Instructors can be found at local yoga studios, health clubs, colleges and universities and the like.

As reported in *Club and Resort Business Magazine*, at the Country Club at Mirasol in Palm Beach Gardens, Fla., a variety of classes are offered for members of all demographics. "We range from classes for the 'young and fit' at 6 a.m. to stretching in the afternoons, a kids class on the weekend, and targeting people with illnesses, like osteoporosis," says Rosa Barksdale, Group Fitness Coordinator. For older populations, Mirasol offers training classes for dementia and Parkinson's disease. Run by a kickboxing instructor who specializes in that type of personal training, the classes include shadowboxing for eye-hand coordination, and incorporate leg-pattern movements that keep the disease from progressing." https://clubandresortbusiness.com/2017/04/group-hustle/.

In addition to a variety of equipment and classes, members are asking for more personal training. Clubs need to be able to provide adequate personal training for a diverse group of members of all ages. To generalize, younger members are likely to want either strength training or to train for an event, such as a triathlon. Older members are likely to want training to help maintain strength, increase flexibility and fight bone loss. As a result, trainers should have experience working with all age groups.

Fitness programmes are becoming an essential component of clubs. We should also add that they can also be revenue generators either through stand-alone fitness memberships or by offering fee based programmes.

Sailing

Yachting, or sailing, is also changing as are most other sports. According to one sailor, the contemporary sailing context is changing to meet the needs of a changing demographics and diverse market with increased sports and leisure offerings available and less time to do them. We have talked about how activities like golf may take upwards of four hours but sailing can fill a full day, or days. The combination of the time required with peoples' time constraints is affecting the way that people approach the sport. Multiple managers mentioned to us that the sport is on the decline because of the time commitment required – at the very least, growth in the sport is flat.

Further, it is a sport that requires skill and, in most cases, a significant financial commitment. In addition, unlike golf or tennis, sailors are required to have at least one certification, showing proficiency on the water. One example of this would be a Pleasure Boaters Certificate which is required in Canada and entails passing a government administered test. US Sailing, which is the governing body in the US, oversees certification, among other things. Their mission states "As the National Governing Body for the sport of sailing, US Sailing's mission is to provide leadership for the sport of sailing in the United States." Similar associations exist in other countries including the Royal Yachting Association (UK), Sail Canada, Australian Sailing and the Yachting Association of India. Each of these associations strives to promote sailing and represent sailors' interests. And most oversee certification programmes of one kind.

Sailing is a sport that has something of a reputation as an exclusive activity. Much of this is owed to events such as the America's Cup, Canada Cup, Newport Bermuda Race, and other major 'regattas' (or races). The cost to enter a boat into one of these competitions can begin at $1 million USD. However, according to Michael Cox, Commodore of the Royal Hamilton Yacht Club (RHYC), many potential and existing members just want to enjoy sailing and the social activities that surround sailing. Thus, yacht clubs offer that opportunity by providing a social venue, water, support, storage, equipment, and increasingly, pools, restaurants, paddle sports and boats. Whereas at one time, most members owned their own boats, clubs are increasingly purchasing boats that members can use for a nominal fee, or in some cases, for the price of membership. For instance, the

Conanicut Yacht Club (in Rhode Island) recently purchased 4 keelboats, for use by its members. Another way that sailors are cutting down on the expense of owning their own boat is to purchase the equivalent of a time share, where boat ownership is spread out amongst multiple owners.

Photo 7.5 : US Sailing # 1. Photo Credit: US Sailing and Matthew Cohen Photography

Sailing attracts people of all ages. Commodore Cox, says that his club has four generations involved in sailing but the population (and membership) is aging. RHYC is aiming for younger demographics but, currently, 70% of its active sailors are over 50 years old. Again, we hear from managers that sailors age out at a certain point, usually as teenagers (because of other demands on their time), and then again in old age (because of loss of ability). Time, money, and skills aside, sailing is another activity that members tend to learn when they are very young. At the Conanicut Yacht Club (in Rhode Island), lessons begin for children as young as 5 years old. Their hope is to instill a love of sailing at an early age. The club offers 150 sessions per season for children as part of a strong junior programme.

Sailing, sail training and racing programmes at yacht clubs are often overseen by a director of sailing, who looks after programming, lessons, safety, staffing, budgets, coaching and promoting sailing as a sport. They would often be supported by a junior sailing director, adult sailing director, coaches, race directors, etc. Depending upon the club, the members (and specifically flag officers such as the commodore and vice commodores) may take a greater or lesser role in the management of the club and events. The director of sailing would work closely with the sailing committee, fleet captain, squadron leaders, commodore and others. In some cases, in very large and active clubs, there would be separate committees for different sailing activities.

Along with lessons, camps, and leisure time sailing, a major activity in yacht clubs is racing (or regattas). Club membership may be composed of some combination of 'cruising' members and 'racing' members. Cruisers are interested in sailing as a social activity, while racers are interested in it for the competition. Most yacht clubs must accommodate both mindsets. Races that are held in clubs may be amongst club members, members of other clubs, or open to the public at large. Larger regattas, as is true with major golf tournaments, bring recognition, prestige, and (sometimes) revenues to the host club. Most importantly though, they create comradery and allow members opportunities to test themselves.

Trends in sailing

Clubs are trying hard to promote sailing, increase interest in the sport and to increase accessibility. One club, the RHYC, has started an initiative to enable children from the community who would typically not be able to afford to sail. They are also offering more programmes for young kids – starting at seven, with comprehensive summer programmes which include parents.

Several associations, as well as clubs, are working to increase access to disabled sailors. One disabled sailing program is known as Able Sail and is offered in various Commonwealth countries. Able Sail programmes are a win-win in for the participants and the club, in that they foster club volunteerism and serve the greater community in a positive manner.

Other strategies for building interest has found clubs working with local college and university sailing teams; developing programmes specifically targeting women (e.g. Women on the Water); and trying simple techniques such as matching new members with more established members.

Perhaps one of the greatest threats (or opportunities depending on how a club responds to meet the needs of the changing sailing context), is the growing popularity of power boats and personal watercraft (PWC). Managers have observed that as members reach a certain age, sailing can become too difficult an endeavor. For this reason, yacht clubs need to find ways to accommodate power boats, although there needs to be a recognition in club operations that sailors and power boaters have very different needs. A successful plan needs to be in place to serve and support both groups. Baby boomers are also attracted to power boats, as, among other things, they require less strength and skill to operate. There are costs associated with each though in addition to the cost of the boat, including gas, docking fees and insurance. That said, many yacht clubs around the world are thriving and there continue be many millions of sailing enthusiasts.

Summary

We conclude by reminding students that we have only discussed a few of the many activities that take place in clubs. Cricket, badminton, squash, polo, curling and bocce continue to be popular around the world and new sports are rising in popularity. Even when we have talked about the declining (or increasing) popularity of a sport, it does not mean that the trend is universal. While it may be declining in one club (or region or country), it does not mean it is declining everywhere. All sports ebb and flow over the generations. Finally, it is important to know a little about each sport as clubs can often house multiple sports under one roof.

Discussion questions

1 Governments usually collect statistics on their citizens' attitudes, behaviours and interests. Find the recent statistics on the most popular recreational activities in your country. Do any of them surprise you?

2 Conduct an inventory of all of the sports offered in private clubs in your area. Which are the most popular? Compare this with popular activities across society. What are the differences and similarities?

3 Why do you think fitness is so popular? What types of fitness equipment/activities/classes are popular at your college or university?

4 Does interest in golf in your area seem to be increasing or decreasing? Conduct an inventory of golf courses in your area (private and public). Do you think there are too many? Too few? Can you estimate what the fair market value for a round of golf is?

References

Cardio Tennis (2018), www.cardiotennis.com

Chambers Company (2018), http://clubviewblog.com/poolside-necessities/

Club and Resort Business (2018), https://clubandresortbusiness.com/2016/07/all-together-now/

Club and Resort Business (2018), https://clubandresortbusiness.com/2017/04/group-hustle/

Hurdzan, M. (2005), *Building a Practical Golf Facility*. American Society of Golf Course, Architects: Brookfield, WI.

International Tennis Federation (2018), www.itftennis.com

Snellinger, R. (2018), http://clubviewblog.com/private-club-pools-create -membership -value/

8 Marketing and Membership

Introduction

Students will often hear that membership is the lifeblood of clubs. This simply means that without members, clubs would cease to exist. This is true for both not-for-profit and for-profit clubs. The focus of this chapter is on membership, that is, who are the members and why do they join; and marketing, that is club activities directed at retaining existing members and recruiting prospective members. The reason that we are combining a discussion of marketing with one of membership, is because it is hard to separate the two functions in clubs. When we use the word 'marketing', we are referring to marketing to members, either current or prospective. At one time, marketing was not within managers' lexicon. However, as we have alluded to several times, clubs must be much more outwardly focused now than they were a generation ago. We will talk more about marketing, but let's first examine why members join clubs.

Why members join clubs

Membership in clubs offers many advantages, albeit at a cost. The reasons that are generally given for joining a club include: 'to golf', 'to network', 'to get ahead in business', 'because my father was a member'. Other reasons that people join clubs, which they might not readily admit, would include prestige, status, peer pressure, conformity, or to reward themselves.

Jim Butler, CCM, CEO of ClubBenchmarking, has delved deeply into this area while looking at the relationships among motivations for joining, member satisfaction, and member loyalty. In his research (https://lib.dr.iastate.edu/etd/15886), he begins by looking at members' motivations for joining a club (and remaining as members or leaving). Dr. Butler examines member motivations for joining from a couple of perspectives. First, he suggests that there are both external and internal drivers that motivate people to join clubs. Examples of external drivers include facilities, the environments (including weather), the club culture, and other characteristics of the club (including reputation).

In addition to these external factors, members also have internal reasons for joining including the ability to relax, socialize, receive high levels of personal service and to enjoy certain health benefits.

Using slightly different terminology, Dr. Butler suggests that there are usually a combination of 'push' and 'pull' reasons prompting a member to join a club. Push factors (member driven) are those factors which meet members' needs and can include some of those listed above: socializing, business, health, athletic activities, etc. Pull factors (club driven) are tangible aspects/features of the club and can include: facilities, weather, reputation and events offered. In one case study, Jim found that the landscaping (and related factors) was actually the main thing that newer members liked about the club and which prompted them to join. This came as a surprise to some of the longer-tenured members.

Finally, Dr. Butler points out that motivators can be different for different demographics groups – men, women, baby boomers, Generation X, etc. Society is often guilty of making generalizations about entire cohorts when, in fact, sub groups within cohorts may exist. One example of this is discussed in an article exploring 'younger' and 'older' members. In her research, Knutson (2001) found significant differences in the behaviours of club members between 50 and 64 and those 65 and older.

The reason that these factors are so important is that managers can use this information to better understand what attracts members to their club, current member needs in determining which services to offer, and how and to whom to market them. Ideally, the ability to capitalize on this information will increase member satisfaction, loyalty, and retention.

The membership process

After a prospective member become sufficiently motivated to apply, two things must happen for them to become a club member – the process is similar in most clubs.

In for-profit clubs, membership applications are made directly to the appointed staff person, who may be the general manager, membership director, or in one club we know of, the director of golf. Regardless of whom the point of contact is, interviews are conducted, the candidate's background is vetted and then the decision is made by a staff member or the owner.

In not-for-profit clubs, it is quite different. In more exclusive clubs, direct applications/letters of interest are discouraged or simply not accepted. Instead, prospective members must be referred, that is nominated, by a current member who serves as a sponsor. From there, the process goes through a series of steps. Some clubs require an additional sponsor while others require multiple sponsors. Then, a complete application is filed including personal references. The entire packet then goes to a membership committee, which vets the candidate by calling references, checking the candidate's background (including a credit check) and considers the general eligibility of the candidate. During this process, the candidate will be interviewed. Also, some clubs will 'post' the fact that a certain candidate is under consideration and invite the general membership to comment on their eligibility. If enough members (or even one in some cases) object to the candidacy, the application will not move forward.

Remember, too, from Chapter 3 that a candidate must first meet the basic threshold for admission. For instance, a candidate will need a university degree for admission to a university club, be of a certain age, work in the appropriate profession, etc. Finally, one membership criteria that most clubs have is that members must be of 'good character' however the club chooses to define it.

After the vetting stage is over, the membership committee moves the packet forward (or not) with a recommendation to either a secondary committee or, in most cases, it goes directly to the board of directors which votes on the candidacy. Admittance is accompanied by a letter of approval to the candidate, an information packet and an invoice for the initiation fee, first month's dues, and whatever other up-front fees are applicable.

Sometimes it is not as straightforward as this. For clubs with waiting lists, gaining admittance will only put the candidate at the bottom of the list, which can represent an additional wait of up to five years or more. Other clubs may have a policy where the candidate is first admitted as a social member (with limited privileges) for a year or more before they are again considered for full admission.

Finally, there is another staff member within the organization who sometimes plays a greater or lesser role in the process but is becoming increasingly important in clubs – that is the position of membership director (sometimes called the marketing and membership director). They may have as central a role as actively recruiting members, to one of just processing the paperwork and orienting new members – it varies from club to club. More will be said about the role of this position later in the chapter.

Membership categories

Often when we think of clubs, we think of a homogeneous group of people, all interested in the same things. In most clubs, this could not be further from the truth (reflect back on the different reasons that members join clubs in the first place). We have already discussed how clubs may have a diverse membership, particularly with respect to age, religion, tenure, interests, net worth and gender. If all members were the same, with the same interests, clubs could charge the same entrance fees, dues, etc. for all of its members. But for most clubs, marketing begins with the ways in which members are segmented within the club – by membership category. We will see the usefulness of segmenting members in this way shortly but, for now, understand that having different membership categories (into which members can be recruited) serves clubs in two primary ways. It allows clubs to (1) maximize its revenues and (2) use its resources efficiently. Also, it allows the member some flexibility in choosing the category that best meets their interests and preferences, which is a marketing tactic. First, though, let's review some of the more common membership categories that exist in clubs.

When members are recommended for membership, it is often with a type of membership in mind. Member owned clubs (country, yacht, city, etc.) will usually have multiple categories. Some may have as few as three or as many as 30. A club with a singular focus (such as a golf or racquet club) may have just a couple of categories, segmented by age.

The most common category, the most expensive, and the one with the most privileges is known as the *full membership* category. Full members pay the highest initiation fees, have extensive privileges, such as having unlimited golf at a country club, and are allowed to vote and hold office. In member-owned clubs, full members make up the majority of equity owners of the club. They are also eligible for committee and/or board membership. Their privileges may or may not be extended to additional family members. In fact, sometimes there is a Family Membership option within this category.

Social memberships typically cost less than full memberships (both in initiation fee and dues) and members do not have full club privileges – that is, they may be allowed to eat in the dining rooms, use the pool and tennis courts, but have limited access to the golf course. They are typically not allowed to vote or serve on committees or the board of directors. These memberships are often filled by members who have friends at the club, and who might live nearby, but do not play golf or otherwise participate in the main athletic activity offered at the club.

Senior memberships are reserved for those who have been members at the club for a long period of time. Clubs usually have a formula that they use to determine eligibility – usually some combination of years of membership and age of the member (for instance, 75 years old and 30 years as a member). Senior members, having formerly been regular members, usually retain all rights and privileges of membership but at reduced dues. There are some concerns that as the population continues to age, clubs may not be able to financially afford a large number of members in this category.

Junior memberships are reserved for members under a specific age (usually between 24 and 39). They have reduced initiation fees and dues, are not eligible for office, have reduced privileges and generally become eligible for full membership once they come of age. In addition, an *Intermediate membership* is available at some clubs and is similar to junior membership but for older members. For instance, a junior membership may run from ages 24 to 29 and an intermediate membership from 30 to 39. Clubs have found that both of these memberships are an excellent way of cultivating future full dues paying members.

Non-resident memberships are restricted to those members who live a certain distance from the club (usually between 100 and 200 km away from the club or outside of the province or state). Sometimes there is also a time restriction, which is to say that members must live in their other residence (away from the club) for a minimum of 6 months. This membership category is often reserved for long-time members who have retired to another area but want to retain a membership, although the rules vary quite a bit from club to club. The membership is usually accompanied by lower fees and dues as well as reduced privileges. Members in this category may have multiple memberships, at different clubs.

Surviving spouse memberships are partially an artifact from the days when men held the sole membership and their wives or partners were guests. A surviving spouse membership allows for the transfer of the membership to the spouse, upon the death of the primary member, given certain restrictions.[1]

Athletic memberships are usually found in country clubs that have extensive athletic facilities and want to 'carve out' categories for members who only want to play tennis (or other racquet sports), swim, or use the fitness center. Dues are

---

1 Clubs are currently revisiting membership categories as these, which, historically, have tended to discriminate against women, single members, divorced members and/or members in domestic partnerships or same sex relationships.

reduced and privileges are limited. Members in this category usually do not have voting rights or the ability to hold office, although this is not true at all clubs. These memberships are particularly effective for clubs to manage usage across club activities.

Honorary memberships are different than the other categories discussed above. These are reserved for heads of state, or persons of notable achievement. They are proffered by invitation or tradition, and come with extensive privileges, no fees and members are not expected to serve on boards or committees. The news media in the USA has been reporting on clubs offering President Obama honourary memberships, since leaving the presidency. One such club is the Beverly Country Club outside of Chicago. Prince William was recently offered an honourary membership at the Marylebone Cricket Club. And past winners of the Masters golf tournament are made honourary members of Augusta National Golf Club. The Rideau Club, in Ottawa, historically has offered honourary memberships to the Governor General of Canada, the Prime Minister of Canada and the Chief Justice of Canada, among others. It is not uncommon for honorary members to rarely, or never, appear at the club at which they are a 'member'.

Corporate memberships are also different from the other types. Some clubs offer corporate memberships to companies that are well represented in their membership ranks. For instance, a club in Sydney, Australia which may have a lot of members from the financial services sector, may offer corporate memberships to companies within that sector. This provides a couple of benefits for the club and the institution. First, it is a way of offering a discounted rate to a company for its loyalty and will typically be for a pre-determined number of company employees, (for instance, four). Second, it may have the built-in flexibility of allowing a new executive with the company to replace one who has been transferred or retired. In essence, many corporate memberships amount to group memberships and may have reduced rates and/or privileges.

There are a host of other types of memberships at different clubs. Some golf clubs may simply have a tiered membership structure titled gold, silver and bronze, with decreasing levels of use. Others may offer family or individual memberships, while other clubs will offer any number of combinations to try to accommodate members. And other clubs may offer seasonal memberships which tend to be less selective.

A recent trend in clubs, particularly for-profit clubs, has been to offer trial memberships, that is, memberships that can be purchased for a short duration (typically one year) at a reduced rate. Usually the dues are higher but the initiation fee is waived. After the trial period expires, the member is able to decide whether to become a full dues paying member or not. Clubs have found that this type of membership can be effective for recruiting new members and generating revenue.

In an excellent article from *Boardroom Magazine*, an industry panel explored the changing landscape of club membership categories:

> *In the original days of the private club industry, clubs essentially, had one class of membership... "you're either a member or you are not", explained Steve Graves, president of Creative Golf Marketing, a company specializing in membership development strategies. "Private clubs had one membership where everyone paid the same joining fee, the same monthly dues and enjoyed the same privileges of membership. Those days are over and the private club industry now offers many types of membership with different joining fees, different monthly dues and different usage privileges...clubs are attempting to offer too many memberships. There is the attempt to meet the needs of each current member or prospective member for fear of losing their dues income. Clubs are throwing a lot of spaghetti against the wall hoping a few strands stick without a true understanding of the unintended consequences of their decisions,"*

http://boardroommagazine.com/what-are-the-trends-for-private-club-memberships-what-should-clubs-be-offering/.

The message here is that there is both risk and reward in offering yet one more additional membership category. However, clubs need to be strategic about how they construct their membership categories.

501(c)7 clubs should be aware of potential tax consequences of different membership categories (IRS Publication 557). Mitchell Stump succinctly states that: "Thus, if there is not a clear relationship of dues to benefits received, the IRS could deem Annual Members to be dealing with the 'general public', arguing that the only reason to have Annual Members is to subsidize Equity Members." He goes on to state that, "However, a difference in dues or fees does not result in inurement if there is a reasonable basis for the difference, such as when the classes of Members have different rights to use Club facilities or Club assets." (Club Tax, 2018).

We want to make one last point regarding membership classifications – if done correctly, it will be legal, have no tax consequences, maximize revenues and satisfy members. If poorly constructed, it can be burdensome (with too many categories), reduce potential revenues, and a club could (conceivably) be penalized. Clubs with complicated spreadsheets to help them organize the various membership categories probably have too many. Clubs with one or two, probably have too few.

Trends in membership

One of the reasons that clubs are so focused on marketing and membership is that growth is not occurring at the same rate that it has in the past. Demographics, the economy, and greater competition (from clubs as well as public accommodations) have all diverted potential club members from joining clubs. A survey of European clubs conducted by Global Golf Advisors found that an approximately equal number of clubs responded that their club's total membership has increased, decreased or remained the same over the previous 5 years, suggesting that growth is essentially flat across the industry.

In the USA, PKF conducts an annual economic study of clubs. In 2018, PKF reports that membership in clubs has rebounded but, at the same time, the number of clubs that are closing exceeds the number of clubs that are opening. Their overall assessment is that country clubs are experiencing a 'stagnant membership base' while city clubs are showing slight growth. Almost every study of clubs that we have seen makes one common pronouncement and one common recommendation: that the high growth period is over and that clubs need to put more of an emphasis on marketing, particularly to historically under-represented groups.

Marketing

Marketing in clubs is a multi-faceted approach to creating customers (or members), communicating with them, giving them what they want, engaging them and retaining them as customers (or members). As we stated earlier, it begins with having the right membership categories, and an appropriate number, which constitutes one part of a club's marketing strategy. In the end, an effective marketing strategy, even in not-for-profit clubs, will result in a net positive cash flow.

The reason that marketing is such an important activity is because membership, across categories, has been decreasing (or, at best, remaining stagnant). Prospective members are different than traditional members and newer/younger members need to be communicated with differently. All of this speaks to how and why clubs have been trying harder to reach out to current members and prospective members. Lest we focus too much attention on attracting new members, it is equally important to try to retain current members, and in fact, can be more cost effective if one considers the lifetime spending of a current member juxtaposed against the cost of recruiting a new member.

The purpose of marketing in clubs is to increase participation and revenue. There are six primary ways that clubs can increase revenue: (1) encourage current members to use the club more frequently; (2) raise prices; (3) get current members to move into a more expensive membership category; (4) attract new members; (5) sell products and services to nonmembers and; (6) add new products and services. Marketing in clubs is directed at accomplishing all of these things and can be divided into three primary types; internal marketing; external marketing; and digital marketing (which encompasses the previous two). Internal marketing focuses on getting more engagement from your current members, which usually results in additional revenue, and longer tenured members. External marketing focuses on attracting new members, or generating business from nonmembers. Digital marketing (including social media) is a method of achieving internal and external marketing objectives but is important enough that it warrants a separate discussion.

Internal marketing

Clubs have always practiced internal marketing – in its simplest form, it is a matter of communicating with members. In days of old, this was accomplished through the club's (usually) monthly newsletter, by posting notices around the club for upcoming events, and by verbally promoting the club and its members, and activities. While clubs continue to do all of these things, the ways that they do them have shifted. Hard copy newsletters, which (some) members continue to rely upon, are now digitized and emailed to members (however, some clubs continue to make hard copies available for members who want them). Web sites are no longer static and are more interactive, allowing members to engage. And social media has been embraced by clubs (Facebook, LinkedIn, Instagram and Twitter seem to be the preferred media). Together, clubs attempt to communicate to, engage with and influence the behaviour of their members through these various channels.

We could give numerous examples of clubs communicating with members – promoting events is probably the most common. Imagine that a manager from Maine (where American lobster is the state crustacean) moves to New Orleans (where crawfish is the state crustacean). She wants to share her love of lobster with the members of her new club so she establishes Lobster Night on a slow night of the week, in an effort to boost business. How will she promote it? Through what channels? How can she get members excited about it? Those are just some of the marketing challenges associated with introducing a new service, program, or event. Clubs are constantly faced with balancing old traditions with new programs and services. Internal marketing is the means of determining: demand for these new services, to whom to target them, and how to communicate them.

External marketing

Where internal marketing is focused on increasing current member engagement, external marketing is focused on markets outside of the current club membership. This, further, can be directed to one of two places: communicating with prospective members in the hopes of recruiting them as members; and marketing to nonmembers for revenue generating business, such as events. We will focus on recruiting new members, which is approached differently by for-profit and not-for-profit clubs. For-profit clubs are not limited by any legal restrictions so may use paid advertising (or social media, etc.) in an attempt to attract new members. And they do. For-profit clubs were a few years ahead of not-for-profit clubs in this respect and continue to be more aggressive than not-for-profit clubs.

One of the most important components of clubs' recruiting efforts has been the creation of (or broadening of) the relatively new position of membership director. The membership director is tasked with increasing recruitment of new members and retention of existing members. In for-profit clubs, membership directors are able to go out into the community and actively recruit. Some clubs even purchase traditional advertising, such as advertisements in newspapers or on websites. Not-for-profit clubs must be mindful of the extent of external outreach, because of their tax status. However, research study after research study shows that the best source of new members are a club's current members. Many clubs are able to leverage their current membership base to attract new members. Some clubs offer incentives, such as reduced dues. Other clubs have open houses, make connections through local businesses and real estate businesses, etc. For this reason, it is important that the membership director is able to work effectively with current members. But much of the external marketing activity is taking place over social media and other forms of digital marketing.

Digital marketing

Digital marketing spans both internal marketing and external marketing so must be discussed on its own. Clubs are now much more adept at pushing their message out, whether it is a general shout out to members, an email blast about an upcoming golf tournament, a tweet about tee-times, or celebrating a star employee. We have already mentioned several social media platforms that clubs are using to communicate their message. In addition to those already mentioned, clubs are also using Snapchat (for geo-targetting), YouTube (for posting videos, such as golf demos and also to allow members to follow channels and brands); Vimio (similar to YouTube, but more for higher quality productions – used by professional photographers and for more creative work); and Pinterest (in large part for weddings) are all also being utilized by clubs.

Being late comers to social media, clubs are and were challenged to leverage social media effectively. As a result, over the last several years, clubs have begun to employ communications managers whose primary job is to manage club communications including monthly newsletters, the website, mobile apps and social media. Sometimes this job will be combined with duties relating to events and membership, but more and more clubs are creating specialized positions limiting responsibilities to managing communications.

Lest the employees in these positions be left to their own devices, several companies have emerged over the last few years to assist clubs in the management of communications, management of their web sites, and particularly, management of social media. One of the prominent companies is MembersFirst, based in Massachusetts. According to their website, "MembersFirst is an award winning digital agency & software provider for member-based organizations, including country clubs, yacht clubs, gated community HOAs, alumni associations, and other private recreational clubs. Through extensive in-house services and a strategic network of technology partners, MembersFirst is the only single-source vendor to offer effective web & print design, value-proven marketing services, cinematic video production, and intelligent software that spans the gamut from simple court reservations to enterprise-level performance reporting" (www.membersfirst. com). Other companies providing similar services include: Jonas, NorthStar, ClubEssential, ForeTees and WebCreative UK.

Sean Bleyl is a former club manager and now Client Development Executive - Eastern Region for MembersFirst. He shared some of his thoughts on the growing use of social media in clubs. Clubs contact MembersFirst (or similar companies) when they realize that they need help engaging members or better communicating their brand. Typically it is the marketing/ membership/communications person, or the person who is in charge of 'lead generation', who makes the initial contact with the company. Sean says that the first wave of clubs using social media started about five years ago and that those clubs still seem to be ahead of the curve. There has since been a second wave over the last couple of years, mostly including clubs that are considered more traditional and were hesitant to embark on social media in earlier stages. One of the reasons that clubs might hesitate, in addition to their concern for member privacy, is their concern about how their members will (or won't) embrace it. According to Sean, even members at traditional clubs are becoming more engaged with social media. In Sean's estimation, all clubs are on social media whether they acknowledge it or not and that clubs need to decide if they want to "create the conversation, be part of the conversation" or just be observers. In other words, more and more clubs are realizing that they want to be able to manage their presence on social media.

As more clubs gain more experience with social media, clubs are moving away from just providing traditional marketing content (just the facts) to providing more interesting content; by telling stories and telling in-depth stories, at that. One company, Storyteller media + communications helps clubs do just that, by helping them with their marketing plans.

Sean goes on to suggest that utilizing different social media platforms gives clubs the opportunity to present the same content but in different ways. Not every club needs to be on every platform, but Sean says that a common mistake occurs when clubs cut and paste content from one platform to another, when the message needs to be tailored to suit a particular platform. Sean's final thought concerned the people who are put in charge of social media at a club. Often it is the director of communications. Whoever it is, Sean suggests that the person needs to be able to use social media from a brand perspective, not just as a user. He added that some companies in the marketplace, such as HubSpot, provide social media training and certification programmes for staff in these positions.

So far, we have used the term 'digital marketing' to refer to the digital channels by which clubs reach prospective (or current) members. A new term now being used in the industry is 'inbound marketing'. This is content marketing that members gravitate to; the thinking goes that if content is of interest to members, it will be of interest to their friends and others in their networks. Inbound marketing blends internal and external marketing with digital marketing. A blog from the Storytellers web site puts it this way: "Changing the way you market your club means moving away from traditional tactics and shifting your focus to a long-term sustainable digital strategy. It means taking your marketing from offline channels (brochures, events, direct mail, door hangers, etc.) and applying online principles... It means powering your website with an abundance of valuable resources (content) to help your website visitors advance their buying decisions." https://blog.storytellermn.com/ccm/outsiders-perspective-private-club-marketing

The trend seems to be toward more of an integrated marketing strategy, in which digital marketing plays a more prominent role.

Membership director

We have referred to the position of membership director a couple of times already. Given the new orientation toward membership recruitment and marketing, the membership director has become an important position in most clubs. This position's primary responsibility is to oversee the management of membership (current and future) by helping to develop and implement membership and marketing goals and initiatives. Again, we need to make the distinction between their roles in for-profit clubs and not-for-profit clubs. In for-profit clubs, where there are no restrictions on advertising and where there is no membership committee, the role of the membership director may be quite broad ranging from establishing sales goals, to identifying prospects, to orienting new members, to overseeing marketing collateral, including the club's web-site. In not-for-profit clubs, their primary responsibility may be more in the way of supporting the general manager and the admissions committee in the areas of maintaining the membership database, member engagement, new member orientation, social media (in the absence of a communications person) and the like. Depending upon the size of the club, there may be an entire membership department or a single individual. If there is a sales and membership department, with multiple positions, events, communications, and membership responsibilities may be separated. In smaller clubs, these positions will be combined.

Even though this has become a critical position in clubs, that has not prevented clubs from enlarging the position, sometimes giving membership directors seemingly unrelated responsibilities. In some cases, this has diluted their effectiveness. Other observers have noticed this too. An article in *Private Club Advisor* (February 2018), discusses how the position can be made to be more effective. It states:

> Consultant Steve Graves is a big fan of membership directors and their
> function in bolstering membership numbers in clubs. "The private club
> industry has been improving because of these talented professionals,"
> Graves declared during the World Conference on Club Management last

year. As an expert in membership marketing, Graves has ideas about how clubs can allow their membership directors to function more effectively. Graves believes the membership director should (1) be more a facilitator and less a recruiter and (2) play a significant role in member retention... Members find new members, he emphasized. A membership director facilitates the sale of memberships. "The membership director produces a game plan for successful membership development—which includes retention." (Private Club Advisor, February 2018).

A membership director with the proper skills and abilities will be able to be involved with every aspect of the membership cycle (recruiting, engaging, and retaining). They should be able to market internally and externally, using whatever means are most effective – which may be a combination of traditional communications with older members and social media with younger ones. Membership directors (and/or communications directors) need to be able to interact effectively with the board, general managers and subordinate staff. And, if the club is active in social media, they need to be well versed in the various platforms. Membership directors are integral to the marketing and membership programmes in clubs but clubs need to clearly delineate their responsibilities. A job description for the membership director at the University Club of Boston is presented in Appendix A.

Going forward

To conclude, clubs now fully recognize the importance of keeping current members happy while maintaining an active marketing program to replace outgoing members with new members. Current members want their club to be seen as a 'fun place'. Marketing (and quality products and services) can reinforce this message/image. Clubs further recognize that newer/younger members want different things from the club experience and that they need to be reached differently than previous generations.

Millennials are getting a lot of attention from clubs, as many clubs see them as being the answer to their future. This perspective is affecting how clubs are reaching out to millennials; it is affecting their services mix; and, in some cases, the culture of clubs. An article about attracting millennials (in *Club Management Magazine*, March/April 2017) highlights a study conducted by CMAA which found that millennials are interested in the following:

- Flexibility in paying initiation fees
- Customized membership options

- Convenience to home and work
- Opportunity to bring guests to the club
- Well-maintained grounds and facilities
- Programs and activities for children
- Opportunity to interact with others of similar interests
- A private place where they can spend leisure time
- Feeling that they are part of a community
- Personal and professional networking
- Prestige and exclusivity in member events
- Members-only events tailored to them
- Fewer restrictions on dress and phone/computer use

(How to attract millennials to your club, 2017)

The good news is that clubs are becoming much more adept in marketing that they were a generation ago, and are learning to leverage social media to their advantage. Further, there is a ready and willing group (millennials) waiting to hear their message. Clubs are also changing to become more flexible in the services that they offer and how they make them available.

As we have pointed out in this chapter, marketing is essential to clubs in the 21st century. As a result, current and future managers should be aware of the many resources available to clubs and club managers, with marketing and membership expertise. Some companies have already been mentioned. Additional resources include:

- The Professional Club Marketing Association (PCMA). Their website says describes the association as "PCMA is the association for membership and marketing professionals at private clubs and is dedicated to providing contemporary resolution to complex club membership and marketing issues through information, education and networking."

- Private Club Advisor is a "monthly business letter written for general managers, owners, operators and board members of private clubs. The letter is designed to educate and inform decision makers of private clubs on industry trends, governmental regulations, recommended policies, best practices and more. The simple and condensed four-page format creates a quick and efficient resource that keeps club executives up to date on relevant, important and helpful information to ensure a more effective decision – making process." Many of the newsletters include membership and marketing content.

- Global Golf Advisors provides advisory services to clubs, in addition to several other types of organizations. They also provide an online blog that might be of interest to students.

- Creative Golf Marketing is "a boutique firm that provides customized marketing and consultation services for the private club industry." They also publish the Club Connection, an online blog.

Summary

In conclusion, much of the attention in clubs (and in industry resources) is on marketing and membership, social media, digital marketing, attracting millennials, and member communications. And the membership director is at the centre of these initiatives. Sandra Petti, Membership/Marketing Manager of Nashawtuc Country Club sums it up well: "Membership directors are a pivotal part of the management team at the club. They are the first person that a prospect connects with and often the only person they know at the club initially. It is the role of the membership director to not only assist with the membership application process, but also to properly orient a new member to ensure that they are connecting with the club and other members. Membership Directors often have the pulse of the membership. The Membership Director is not only the face of the club, but also acts as the member's oldest friend, as members share good experiences and even less than perfect experience with them. The Membership Director is the bridge between the members and other departments so that the club can operate harmoniously."

Discussion questions

1 How do you think marketing is different in clubs than in other types of hospitality organizations?

2 In your experience, do you see evidence that clubs rely on one form of marketing over another?

3 Give some examples of club marketing activities that you have observed. In each instance, how was effectiveness measured?

References

Boardroom Magazine (2018) what are the trends for private club memberships? What should clubs be offering? boardroommagazine.com/ what-are-the-trends-for-private-club-memberships-what-should-clubs-be-offering/.

Butler, J. (2017) Predicting loyalty in clubs through motivation, perceived value, satisfaction, and place attachment https://lib.dr.iastate.edu/etd/15886/.

Club Management Magazine (2017). How to attract millennials to your club.

Global Golf Advisors (2018), https://www.globalgolfadvisors.com/wp-content /uploads/2017/11/11-27-17-European-ClubTrends_BestPractices-Master -FINAL-v2.pdf.

Knutson, B. (2001). Mature club members; Are they a homogeneous or heterogeneous market? *Journal of Hospitality and Leisure Marketing*, **9**(1/2), 35 – 51.

Private Club Advisor (February 2018). www.privateclubadvisor.com

Storytellers, https://blog.storytellermn.com/ccm/outsiders-perspective-private -club-marketing

Stump, M. (2018). Club Tax. https://clubtaxnetwork.com

Appendix A: Membership Director, University Club of Boston

Job summary

Develop and implement programs, projects and activities designed to increase and retain membership in the club. Also acts as supervisor for the Women's Locker Room staff of 4.

Responsibilities:

- Maintains the club's data base (membership register) of members' files.
- Develops and ensures that established procedures for processing prospective members' applications are consistently followed.
- Plans and implements strategies to meet club membership goals.
- Processes all requests for resignations and leaves of membership.
- Assists prospective members in fulfilling application requirements.
- Conducts orientation meetings with new members.

- Calls and requests active members to make personal referrals and to assist with recruitment efforts.
- Processes member resignations; develops reports and undertakes special projects as applicable if membership retention problems arise.
- Manages locker room locker assignments
- Assesses the need for and makes recommendations regarding membership classifications to help ensure that the needs of ever-changing markets are met.
- Personally meets each club member and instills confidence that the club is operated in the best interests of the membership.
- Serves on admissions committees to assure members' interests are consistently addressed.
- Conducts tours for prospective members.
- Tracks the success and overall performance of all membership activities.
- Coordinates all club public relations efforts, members' newsletters, news and media events and club brochures.
- Attends management and staff meetings.
- Effectively responds to member comments in accordance with club standards, policies and rules; uses ideas, feedback and suggestions to continuously improve the services provided to members.
- Develops and adheres to a departmental budget; after approval, monitors and takes corrective action as necessary to help assure that budget goals are attained.
- Recruits, trains, supervises, schedules and evaluates subordinates according to established club procedures.
- Plans and develops training programs and professional development opportunities for herself and all other subordinates.
- Reports approved new members to the controller to initiate proper administration of their memberships; ensures that applications are completely and properly filled out, that initiation fees are collected and that new members understand the privileges and costs of becoming a member.

9 Financial Operations in Clubs

Introduction

Most students have taken a module in accounting, finance or both. There are many aspects of both of these areas (and where they overlap) that apply to clubs. In this chapter, we will present the areas with which students should be familiar, and those which club managers have told us are important.

This chapter will focus primarily on 'big picture' financial topics, that is, financial areas that are under the purview of the general manager, finance committee, controller, and/or the board of directors. However, club practices differ from those of other hospitality organizations in both large and small ways, many of which affect their financial procedures. For instance, many clubs do not accept cash payments (or credit cards) for services, only allowing members to charge services rendered to their accounts. This obviously impacts who pays, how they pay, cash flows, and systems and procedures. Another example is the importance of dues to clubs – clubs' greatest source of revenues is usually in dues (quarterly or monthly payments by members). This means that clubs rely greatly on a source of funds that is a function of the number of members, not member activity. Another example of how club finances differ is that they have sources of revenues and expenses that are unique in the hospitality industry, such as initiation fees, 'unused food minimums' and 'unrelated business income'. Add to this that the majority of clubs are operated on a not-for-profit basis, meaning that they manage their operations for the long-term sustainability of the organization and not for short term profit. All of this adds up to clubs representing a unique niche in the area of financial management.

Financial management in clubs

When we refer to financial operations in clubs, we are referring to the ways in which clubs price their products and services, generate and collect revenues, incur and pay expenses, manage their cash and assets (including investments), forecast revenues and expenses, and how they document and report all of the above. Some financial practices are industry-wide while others will differ among different types of clubs, most notably between for-profit and not-for-profit clubs.

Much has been written about the financial side of club operations (for instance, one prominent scholar, Dr. Ray Schmidgall has written extensively on accounting practices in clubs). It is important for students to understand financial operations for three primary reasons; (1) The general manager (for those of you who aspire to this position) is the person ultimately responsible for meeting the financial goals of the organization (along with boards of directors); (2) Clubs are much more focused on their financial results now than they were a generation ago; and (3) Not-for-profit clubs, in particular, are governed by a different set of financial rules than are for-profit organizations. For all of these reasons, it behooves students to learn as much as they can about financial management of a club. In this chapter, we will highlight the main areas with which students should be familiar.

Before we proceed however, let's reiterate one of the important traits of clubs that we have mentioned several times thus far. Most clubs that exist are operated on a not-for-profit basis (as 501(c)7s in the USA). This means that their mission is different from for-profit businesses. It also means that their mission is centred around taking care of their members and they are not under obligation to show a profit. Despite this, an understanding of finance (and accounting, and budgeting and related areas) is important for managers to responsibly manage and protect a club's assets, break-even (or generate profit in a for-profit environment), make critical financial decisions, comply with government tax laws, and otherwise use financial knowledge to manage a club over the short-term and the long-term.

Revenues and expenses in clubs
Revenues

The greatest source of funding for most clubs is dues. On an individual basis, members may pay $6,000 USD, or more, per year to retain their club membership. Thus, if a club has 1,000 members (to keep the maths simple), a club could generate $6 million USD per year in dues alone. In total, clubs generally derive 40% or more of their annual revenues from dues (more for country clubs, less for city clubs). For this reason, clubs depend on dues to fund much of the day-to-day activity of the club. So dues income (which is a function of the dues structure, number of members, and member retention) is critically important to clubs.

Other revenue sources may include food and beverage sales, golf fees (greens fees, cart rentals, lessons, etc.), guest fees, selling of function space, and sale of merchandise. This last category could be sizable, depending upon the types of merchandise and the markup (golf and tennis equipment, clothes, etc.). In addition, city clubs might derive revenues from the sale of overnight guest rooms or parking. Yacht clubs might earn extra money from the rental of moorings or dock space, boat rentals and the like. Some clubs also offer fee-based activities such as fitness classes.

In addition to revenues that come from club members (above), clubs may also generate income from nonmembers (known as nonmember income). This occurs when nonmembers use member facilities, which may include any or all of the above. It also includes any income generated by members of reciprocal clubs (after all, reciprocal members are not true members). The difference here is that member-owned, equity clubs (those that are tax exempt), are limited in some countries (for instance by the IRS in the USA) to a certain proportion of nonmember revenue (15%), and it must be accounted for separately. One source of nonmember income that can be quite significant, is hosting an 'outing' for an outside group. This usually entails committing the entire club to the group though, so is not something that is allowed at every club.

Clubs may also receive income from what are known as 'nontraditional business activities', which can include off-premise catering, sale of food and/or wine to members, and long term rentals of guest rooms. This source of revenue, too, must be kept to a minimum lest clubs be at risk of losing their tax exempt status.

Another significant source of revenue is a club's initiation (or joining) fee. This can range from the low $1,000s to into the $100,000s. Because of the size of the fees, as well as the unpredictability, it is usually treated differently from other sources of revenues. Whereas most of the examples given previously go toward funding the operational budget (see below), initiation fees are usually set aside for funding capital projects and depreciation. More will be said about this later.

Finally, an important point must be made regarding the differences among different revenue sources. Some are simply worth more to a club, that is, they have less cost associated with them. For instance, it is often said that dues payments drop directly to the bottom line. That is to say, there is no direct cost associated with collecting dues from members. On the other hand, $100 received from a member for dinner does not represent $100 in profit. After wages, food, and linens have been paid for, there may only be $5 to $10 left over to cover other expenses, or nothing at all.

To summarize, revenues can come from a variety of sources including one time payments (such as sales of assets), ongoing purchases from members and purchases from nonmembers. Donations are also occasionally made to clubs (cash or in kind).

Expenses

On the expenses side, the greatest cost for most clubs is payroll. In some cases, payroll (and related expenses such as un/employment insurance, health insurance and other benefits) can represent between 50% and 60% of a club's total annual budget. This is why it is said that clubs are labour intensive. Clubs employ people in a variety of positions from well-compensated general managers (and other professional staff) to service employees in the clubhouse to grounds crew.

Another major expense for clubs with food and beverage includes the cost of goods sold. For clubs with golf, additional expenses would include course maintenance, including insecticides, pesticides, etc. as well as grass seed, petrol (for machinery), and anything else needed to maintain the golf course on a daily basis.

Other expenses incurred by all clubs would include the cost of real estate (lease payments, rent or mortgage), insurance, interest and depreciation. For-profit clubs would also have associated marketing costs. Taxes would vary from club to club, but those registered as not-for-profit would typically be exempt from paying income taxes.

In a not-for-profit environment, clubs would attempt to break-even, meaning that total revenues and total expenses would be virtually equal. Any surplus would be re-invested in the club or would be invested for later use. Laws in many countries prohibit the distribution of profit to members, such as would be the case in publicly traded corporations which would distribute them in the form of dividends. For-profit clubs' objective would be to show a profit at the end of the year which would be reinvested in the club or be returned to the owner (s).

Clubs often express revenues and expenses as percentages of the total. This is common in individual club financial statements as well as in industry reports. For instance, dues income would be expressed as a percentage of total revenue, and payroll as a percentage of total expenses. It is important to understand revenues for the purposes of increasing (or decreasing) them, analyzing, reporting and controlling them. It is also critical to developing a strong budget. It is important to understand expenses to know where the club is spending its money and when to increase or decrease them.

Budgets

R evenues and expenses come together in the formulation of a budget. Budgets are essentially financial forecasts, based on historical data, and are a way for clubs to plan financially for the future. Managers are responsible for preparing the various budgets for approval by the board of directors (in equity clubs) or for owners (in for-profit clubs). Clubs may have an annual budget of between $1 million USD to over $25 million USD, although some clubs may fall outside of this range. The average club budget, according to ClubBenchmarking, is $7.5 million USD (based upon their subscribers of about 1,000 clubs). Club budgets can be generally broken into three main areas: (1) operations; (2) cash; and (3) capital.

Operations budgets

T he *operations* budget is the short term (monthly, quarterly and annual) budget which focuses on the funding of operations, that is keeping the club operating on a day to day basis. It is a forecast of expected revenues and expenses for a given period in the future, usually one year (with monthly updates). It must take three primary factors into consideration: (1) number of members (including changes in number); (2) demand for services; and (3) expenses. It is important to remember that it is a forecast and that things are likely to change, including but not limited to levels of business fluctuations, weather, the activities mix, economic downturns, new legislation, and cost increases. Some simple examples will illustrate how each of these factors can be affect change and, thus, change the forecast. First, the number of members is not always a constant. During the recession, clubs lost a lot of members. At other times, they may gain new members, for instance after a new membership drive, and this must be factored in. As a result, clubs have a historic net/loss of members that they can use and/or a goal for new memberships for the upcoming period.

Second, managers must create budgets based on demand estimations. This means that, in a golf club, a manager will try to estimate how many golf rounds will be played, how many fee paying guests will play, etc. In the food and beverage area, estimates must be made as to how many members will dine in the restaurants and how many events will be sold. Both of these things change from year to year depending on demographics, weather and the economy and other factors outside of the control of the club.

Finally, as any household consumer knows, costs for products changes with some frequency, whether we are referring to food, petrol, pool chemicals, or wages. As an example, many municipalities in North America are increasing their minimum wages significantly. If a wage increase is scheduled to go into effect on 1 January, this must be built into the budget for the upcoming year.

David Scaer, CCM, General Manager of the Nashua Country Club, describes budgets and the budgeting process as follows: "The budget process is not one single task completed over a short period of time and then only examined at a monthly board meeting. A budget can be living document that can be a useful tool even after the fiscal year has started. One should consider constantly adjusting the budget model throughout the year and using it as a forecast tool. You will never be 100% correct on your budget but staying on top of trends and making adjustments will help establish you as the budget expert in your club-and that is one of the most important factors of being a successful manager... It is too easy to rely on historical data alone without considering membership trends and other factors, and many private clubs use that approach. The first step to budgeting is to predict the number of members the club will have in each category for each month. Having an accurate forecast will aid in budgeting many income and expense lines in the budget. This is done by averaging historical trends and by estimating the type of membership year you anticipate."

The other reason a budget (and tracking of the budget) is important is to investigate any variances between the budgeted item (revenue or expense) and the actual amount that was received (or spent). In this way, managers can track variances, or differences, identify potential problem areas, and make necessary adjustments for the future. In the end, the operations budget serves as a tool for managing the club's financial resources for the year.

To summarize, the operations budget is prepared by the general manager (with help from direct reports), based upon historical information and knowledge of changes that may take place. It is reviewed by the board of directors on a monthly basis, with changes made and justified.

Cash budgets

In contrast, the *cash budget* is prepared to ensure that the club is able to meet its short term (less than one year) cash requirements. The cash budget focuses on estimated cash inflows (dues, sales, etc.) and outflows (payroll, operating expenses, etc.). It is usually prepared on an annual basis (or a shorter time period). In contrast to the operations budget, the cash budget helps a manager manage the cash flow over the short-term. For instance, one general manager told us that there are periods when the inflow of dues subsides because of payment schedules and the club may have to take out a short-term loan to cover immediate expenses. Cash budgets can highlight when these times might occur as well as their severity.

Capital budgets

The *capital* budget is gaining greater attention in clubs. It is so named because it refers to the forecasting of capital needs; that is the future needs in the area of assets (land, building, furniture, fixtures and equipment) and/or the improvements made to them (renovations to the clubhouse or upgrades to the golf course, in the case of a country club). Most clubs that we have visited in recent years have undergone some sort of capital improvement whether it was a clubhouse renovation/rebuild, a golf course reconstruction/redesign, upgrades to irrigation, new tennis courts, new ballrooms, etc. Without exception, each of these projects requires advanced planning, funding and member approval (in equity clubs). A capital budget is different from either the operations or cash budget in a number of ways. First, the layers of approval are much more involved, with committees and the board being heavily invested. For larger, more expensive projects, most clubs will require a vote by the general membership for approval. In nonequity clubs, it simply takes availability of funds and willingness by the owner or developer to make the investment.

The sources of funding can be different as well. We have already mentioned the use of initiation fees as a basis for funding capital projects. However, not all clubs have these fees readily available so clubs some may have to borrow funds or assess (bill) members for the prorated cost of a project. Another option for funding capital projects is becoming more common – that is clubs imposing 'capital dues' which is a regular (dedicated) payment that club members make and is recurring (as opposed to assessments which have a dedicated purpose and limited life). Clubs may also borrow money from a bank or other type of financial institution.

Finally, the timeline for capital budgets (as opposed to operations or cash budgets) is much longer, and may be five years or more. Even then, projects are contingent on a positive vote by members. We know of several major projects which were voted down once, sent back to a committee or management to be reworked, and then brought back to the membership at a later date.

Because of the greater level of expense, risk and the increased planning horizon, clubs must go through an additional step in determining if a capital project is feasible. If one accepts that the value of a monetary unit is worth more in the future than it is now (because of the opportunity to invest it), clubs must calculate the 'time value' of money. Alternatively, they may calculate the present value. In the end, they must find a way to calculate when the project will be paid for. This is based on several factors including the cost of money, sources of funds, and demand.

A final word about capital budgets

Capital budgets have always been an important part of financial planning in clubs. However, they are arguably becoming more important as two important factors converge. First, over the past decade, many clubs' financial resources have become stressed. Within a single club, different projects will necessarily compete for the same valued funds. A simple example of this is clubs which offer both tennis and golf. The tennis players will always want more and better tennis courts while the golfers will always want a new and improved golf course. A budget forces a club to practice forward thinking and make some hard decisions regarding how and where they want to spend their money.

Second, as clubs attempt to recruit new members, having a clubhouse that is up to date, a golf course that is well cared for, and all of the amenities that new members are asking for (fitness centres, pools, etc.), is critical to recruitment. All of this costs money though. Clubs that do not keep their clubs up-to-date, cannot recruit new members, do not receive influxes of new cash, and cannot make the necessary improvements. All of this can result in a downward spiral for the club. While capital budgets cannot solve all of a club's problems, it demands planning, which can prevent many problems.

A recent article in *Private Club Advisor* entitled 'What's Driving Your Budget', offers some thoughts on how budgets are linked to a club's mission:

> *Does your club mission statement drive your club budget or does your club continually compromise its mission to meet budgetary constraints? Eric Gregory, president of Blueprint Club Consulting, believes that while most club mission statements include words like premiere, exceptional, or first-class to describe facilities and services, many clubs fail to present a budget that allows for successful implementation of the mission of the club. "The club's mission should be the driver of the budget, not the other way around," Gregory said. He equates this to wanting champagne on a beer budget. "While lack of interest from potential members may contribute to such a mind-set, clubs must understand that cutting and slashing is not a formula for success. It will only further decrease the club's attractiveness to current and future members."*

Gregory strongly encourages that each committee and board member as well as all managers know the mission and use it as a guide when making operating and capital decisions.

www.privateclubadvisor.com.

Financial statements

At some point, a club must compose financial statements for use and review by owners, boards, committees, tax authorities and/or auditors using much of the information discussed above. The two most common types of statements are the *income statement* and the *balance sheet*, referred to as such in for-profit organizations. In not-for-profits, these are known as the *statement of activities* and the *statement of financial position*, respectively (although some club managers may choose to call them by their more common names).

The *statement of activities* is just that – a statement that reflects how a club performed financially during a period of time – usually a month, quarter or year. In its simplest form, it compares revenues and expenses in an effort to show whether there was a profit (or loss) at the end of the period. This is why these statements are also known as *profit and loss statements*.

We have already reviewed the more common areas of revenue (dues, food and beverage, sports, merchandise sales) and expenses (payroll, cost of goods, operating supplies). Revenues and (operating) expenses represent the first two categories of the statement.

Revenues – Expenses = Income Before Fixed Charges.

Fixed charges (rent, property taxes, etc.), applicable income taxes, other activities (assessment, etc.), and changes in net assets are then listed. The 'bottom line' represents the increase (or decrease) of net assets. (Note: initiation fees may appear in one of two places, depending upon if they are dedicated to the operations or the capital budget).

Also, each line item (such as food and beverage) will have an associated supporting departmental statement to accompany it. These will show the financial activity that took place over the period in the individual departments, with finer detail.

In short, the *statement of activities* breaks down the changes in the operating results over a discreet period of time. It shows managers, and others, whether the club made a profit, or not, and where the revenues and expenses originated from.

This is obviously important information, especially when compared to statements from previous periods.

The *statement of financial position*, in contrast, illustrates the club's financial position at one point in time, usually the end of an accounting cycle. Rather than showing sources of revenues and expenses, it represents what a club owns and what it owes. To contrast the difference, and purpose of the two statements, notice that the statement of activities does not give any indication of whether a club owns any golf carts, or if so, how many. Nor does it give an indication of how many square metres the clubhouse is or how many boats it might own (in the case of a yacht club). The statement of financial position does this by taking account of the *assets* that a club owns. This is the first category in the statement: assets will include cash, investments, inventories and prepaid expenses, and any other items that are considered as having value. Schmidgall identifies the six major components of the assets section as being: current assets, noncurrent receivables, designated assets, investments, property and equipment and other assets. Clubs may own assets of tremendous value, and these are reflected in this part of the statement. Much of this is usually invested in buildings and property. There are clubhouses that are over 10,000 square metres in size. Further, some clubs are located on land that is upwards of 200 hectares. Imagine the worth of a high-rise building in a downtown location, housing a city club. Or a club that owns a 36 hole course. Further, clubs may invest in assets in addition to the land and the building. We have visited clubs that have extensive art collections, and are veritable museums, or libraries with extensive holdings of rare books. But perhaps more common is the investment that clubs make in equipment. In country clubs, this would include golf carts and machinery to maintain the grounds. In yacht clubs, this might include boats. In city clubs (and others), it would include tables, chairs, fixtures and furnishings. All together, the balance sheet indicates the value of such assets.

One of the important principles of understanding the statement of financial position is that the first category (*assets*) must equal the next two categories (*liabilities* and *equity*). *Liabilities* represent how much is owed to third parties and other financial obligations (for example accounts payable, taxes and long-term debt). Finally, where most balance sheets show a category entitled *equity* – in clubs this is known as *unrestricted net assets*, which represent the equity of members.

Together, these two financial statements show the financial position of the club, as they would for a commercial business. They are prepared by the general manager in conjunction with the controller, for feedback and approval by the board of directors.

It is not the purpose of this chapter to instruct students on the preparation and intricacies of these statements. For further information, please refer to the Uniform System of Financial Reporting for Clubs or other good reference sources, which provide examples of the statements discussed.

Taxes[1]

Taxes (or exemption from them) play an important role in every business, and particularly clubs. Even though we have used the term 'tax-exempt' throughout the book, not all clubs fall into this category, and even then it only refers to exemption from income taxes. At the risk of oversimplifying, for-profit clubs (typically owned by an individual, company or developer) pay federal and state/provincial income taxes on any profits that they make. In contrast, member owned clubs are by default, classified as Section 277s (in the USA) unless they file for a tax exemption. If approved for the exemption, they become classified as 501(c)7s and are exempt from paying federal and state income taxes, that is, taxes on any surplus that they might generate by the end of the tax year. However, this scenario is rife with caveats and exceptions.

First, all clubs that receive a tax exemption are restricted and limited to the amount of nonmember income they can receive. This is known as the 15%/35% rule and restricts the percentage of gross revenues that can be derived by non-members (15%) and nonmember revenues plus investment interest (35%). If the club exceeds these limitations it will have to pay taxes on that amount and/or lose its tax exemption. The term 'Unrelated Business Income' (UBI) serves to distinguish between member generated income (exempt income) and nonmember generated income (taxable income).

Some clubs that are classified as 501(c)7s actually decide that it is in their best financial interest to pay taxes. Others do just enough 'outside' business to stay below the 15% threshold. This is a decision that must be made by individual clubs. In countries where the amount of nonmember business is not restricted, clubs may choose to collect a greater portion of nonmember revenues. Certain types, such as those from banquets and catering, can be a good revenue source.

Clubs may also decide to sell assets from time to time, such as land, buildings or artwork. Depending upon the circumstances (largely based upon the timing of re-investment), these sales may be deemed taxable events.

---

1 Note: Much of this section focuses on taxes specific to the US. Students should become familiar with taxes and tax laws specific to the countries that they are working or studying.

It is important to remember that any tax exemption that a club receives, refers to income tax. Clubs are under obligation to pay other forms of taxes including property taxes (although sometimes at a reduced rate), payroll, sales taxes, and other related taxes.

A short word on sales taxes (or VAT) that clubs must pay. This will also vary from region to region but an example from the USA will be provided here. Clubs typically pay sales tax on goods purchased that are not for resale, such as equipment. However, the sales tax on merchandise (clothing, golf equipment, etc.) for which the club is not the end-user and that is sold to members, meals in the restaurants, and overnight room sales is paid by the member, as the member is the end user.

Finally, while not necessarily tax related, the IRS in the USA does require that every not-for-profit club submit a 990-T form at the end of every tax year, which shows their income. The IRS describes the form as such: "Form 990 must be filed by an organization exempt from income tax under section 501(a) (including an organization that has not applied for recognition of exemption) if it has either (1) gross receipts greater than or equal to $200,000 or (2) total assets greater than or equal to $500,000 at the end of the tax year (with exceptions described below for organizations eligible to submit Form 990-N and for certain organizations described in Section B."

Much more could be written about taxes. For an excellent source of tax information in the USA, students should refer to the document the *Club Tax Book*, prepared by Mitchell Stump, CPA.

Performance measures

The final section of this chapter will focus on the tools that managers use to determine how their club is performing, beyond and in addition to the statement of financial position and statement of activities. The common name for performance metrics are 'ratios'. Much of the information for use in ratio analysis is drawn from the information already provided in the statements previously discussed. They help managers to determine the financial health of a club. The reason they are called ratios, is that they are expressed as ratios and are calculated by dividing one numeric value by another.

Students should already be familiar with some simple ratios that are used to measure performance in the hospitality industry. One such measure is *food cost percentage* (cost of food/sales) which is used in restaurants, and clubs, to track the cost of food over time. In addition, a common performance metric used in the hotel business is the *occupancy percentage* (hotel rooms sold/total rooms available) which indicates sales efficiencies. These are just two examples.

There are five accepted classifications of ratios: liquidity, solvency, activity, profitability and operating. According to Schmidgall,

> Liquidity ratios *reveal the ability of a club to meet its short–term obligations.* Solvency ratios...*measure the extent to the club has been financed by debt and is able to meet its long-term obligations.* Activity ratios *reflect management's ability to use the club's assets, while several* profitability ratios *show management's overall effectiveness as measured by returns on sales and investments. Finally,* operating ratios *assist in the analysis of a club's operations.* (Schmidgall and Damitio, 2001, p. 111).

Within the five classifications, there are over 20 accepted ratios that have been used successfully in business, and in clubs, for a very long time. Examples include ratios which measure assets to liabilities, debt-equity ratio, inventory turnover, return on members' equity, and the aforementioned food cost ratio. Our purpose here is not to review and calculate common ratios, but rather to discuss the direction in which the industry is adopting new measures of tracking performance. One company that is leading this effort is ClubBenchmarking.

ClubBenchmarking

ClubBenchmarking is a Massachusetts based company which provides financial expertise to private clubs. In fact, the entire (original) premise of the company was to apply ratio analysis to club finances, using their proprietary platform, and then use that information to benchmark it against industry averages. In this way, CB provides similar services that STR does for the lodging industry. In their own words,

> *"The CB* Financial Benchmarking Platform *is a subscription-based online management tool that allows you to benchmark your club's financial & operational performance against the industry's largest and most accurate standardized database. Our proven Financial Insight Model™ and Key Performance Indicators are the cornerstones of a common and strategic industry framework clubs can use to accurately assess and benchmark their financial and operational health."* (www.clubbenchmarking.com)

The company is taking the concept of ratio analysis, developing ratios that they feel are more suited to measuring performance in the club industry, and benchmarking them against the aggregate data provided by their other subscribers. They typically present their data using charts, dividing their charts into quartiles, and showing where individual clubs compare with industry benchmarks.

They have a total of 20 ratios, or as they call them 'Key Performance Indicators' or KPIs. Some of them look similar to standard industry ratios while others depart greatly from how the industry has historically measured financial performance. To understand the information that their graphics convey, it is important to understand a few of their key terms. A few of the key drivers that CB uses include:

- *Operating revenue*: this equals total revenue generated annually, which funds the operations budget.

- *Gross profit*: this equals dues plus net sales from revenue producing departments. Their premise is that this is a metric because it drives operational health of a club.

- *Gross margin*: this equals gross profit - variable expenses (such as labour cost).

- *Net available capital*: this measure the amount available for capital investment.

- And finally, *net available capital to operating revenue ratio* indicates whether the club is generating sufficient capital for needed projects, current and future.

An example of their depiction of Gross Margin for one club, benchmarked against the industry is shown in Figure 9.1, and their 20 KPIs are shown in Figure 9.2.

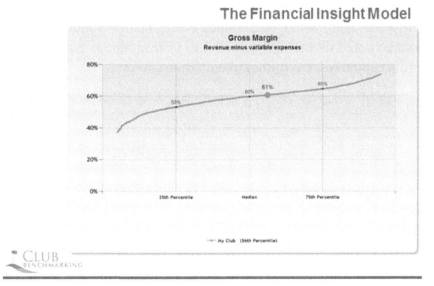

Figure 9.1

The Common KPIs – These Matter to ALL CLUBS (Annual)

Income Statement Operating Ledger	Balance Sheet Capital Ledger
1. Operating Revenue	1. Net Worth Over Time
2. Gross Profit/Gross Margin	2. Equity to Assets and Liabilities to Assets Ratio
3. Sources of Gross Profit	3. Net Property, Plant & Equipment
4. Dues to Operating Revenue Ratio	4. Net PPE to Gross PPE Ratio
5. Fixed Expenses to Revenue Ratio	5. Total Capital Income
6. Proportionate Fixed Expense by Department	6. Net Available Capital
7. Operating Result and Margin	7. Net Available Capital to Revenue Ratio
8. Payroll to Revenue Ratio	8. Debt to Revenue Ratio
9. F&B Profit/Loss as % of Dues Revenue	9. Debt to Equity Ratio
10. Full Member Dues	
11. Full Member Equivalents	

Figure 9.2

Much of the ClubBenchmarking's current emphasis is upon helping managers redirect their attention from being solely on the Income Statement to focusing on the Income Statement AND the Balance Sheet. They believe that many of the financial problems that clubs are facing is due to a lack of capital planning. In presenting information in the way that they do, ClubBenchmarking has a few primary objectives. They want clubs (their clients) to be able to: (1) measure performance in relevant ways that will help them manage their current operations while planning for the future; (2) see how their club benchmarks against the rest of the industry; and (3) help managers better communicate with boards about club finances. It should also be noted that CB is beginning to offer an entire portfolio of services ranging from capital reserve studies to employee surveys.

Summary

We have reviewed only a few of the important financial topics with which students should be familiar including revenues and expenses, budgets, financial statements, taxes and industry metrics. Students will one day find themselves in positions of authority where they will be expected to understand, manage, improve, and communicate the financial operations of a club.

Discussion questions

1 Do most of the clubs in your area operate on a for-profit or not-for-profit basis? How do you think this impacts club operations?

2 Compare Statements of Activity from two different types of clubs. Compare the categories of expenses and revenues. Discuss what factors (internal and external) that might affect the largest revenue sources.

3 After completing the previous question, calculate several ratios for the financial data. What conclusions can you draw from the results?

References

Club Benchmarking (2018), www.clubbenchmarking.com.

Schmidgall, R, and Damitio, S, (2001), *Accounting for Club Operations*, AH&LA, Lansing, Michigan.

What's Driving Your Budget?, (2017). *Private Club Advisor,* November, www.privateclubadvisor.com.

10 Trends in Clubs

Introduction

As we explain to our students, clubs have changed more in the last 10 years than they did in the previous 100 years. While this is perhaps a slight exaggeration, it is close to the truth. For many years, while the economy, legal environment, and demographics were all in their favour, clubs were able to continue managing their organizations as they have always done. Then, as their members grew older (and less active), new tax laws came into play, the economy weakened, and new generations with different needs emerged, clubs either changed of their own accord or were forced to change. When discussing changes in clubs, it is helpful to explore the trends that are occurring.

According to Merriam-Webster, a trend is a "prevailing tendency or inclination." That is to say, trends are waves on which the industry rides. That said, not every trend is apparent in every club. Nor are trends of equal stature or power. Some trends have taken the club industry by storm while others grow more slowly over a number of years.

It is not only important for students to understand the current trends that are shaping the industry but also to learn how to identify future trends as they occur. With regard to the latter, our advice is to network, read the trade publications (such as *Club Management* magazine), attend conferences and other professional development venues, engage on social media (particularly LinkedIn and other professional networks), visit clubs and talk with managers.

Many of these trends have been discussed in earlier chapters but we will summarize some of the more important ones in this chapter, while providing greater context. We have identified ten trends which bear further examination: demographic changes; casualization; recreation; food and beverage; families; reciprocal agreements; technology; governance; capital projects; and the greening of the industry.

Changing demographics

The demographic profile of members is changing, particularly with regard to age and gender. This is critical as it, in itself, is driving many of the other changes that are taking place in clubs. Clubs are actually working against societal changes in this area particularly with regard to age. The aging of the population is well documented: populations in much of the world are aging and this has hurt clubs. Aging is particularly acute in most western countries and Japan: the reverse is true in many middle-eastern countries where the age of the population is actually decreasing.

The club industry has historically relied on the 'older' segment of the market which has the time and disposable income necessary to join a club. However, after many years during which clubs did not have to recruit new (and younger) members, clubs found themselves in a position where (1) older members were dying or moving away; (2) the economy further eroded their member base; and (3) younger members were not replacing former members at an adequate rate. For all of these reasons, clubs are now actively recruiting younger members. As they do, clubs have had to adjust their cultures, service offerings, and prices. This has had a salient effect on clubs and has led to many of the other trends discussed below.

We have also discussed the changes (decrease) in discriminatory policies at clubs against people of colour, certain religions and ethnicities. As clubs embrace members of different backgrounds, they will also have to be more sensitive to other cultures and traditions, which will necessarily impact programmes and services.

Finally, women are taking more prominent roles in clubs. In most clubs, women are now equal partners as far as membership privileges go. This has set off, among other things, a re-writing of club bylaws to better accommodate women. While there still is not equal representation on club boards of directors, women are playing more of a role in decision making in clubs.

Casualization

With each new generation, comes a change in the level of formality and how various customs and traditions are upheld. Generally speaking, younger generations are driving society to be less formal. With few exceptions, clubs are following the trend of becoming more casual. This trend is also occurring in colleges and universities, restaurants, the workplace, and society at large. But what does this actually mean in clubs? First, it has affected the way people dress in the clubhouse, on tennis courts, golf courses and elsewhere. Clubs are beginning to eliminate (or relax) stringent dress codes that once required members to dress in a certain way. It was not that long ago that formal dining rooms in clubs required that male members wear a jacket and tie and that women also dressed comparably. Now, it is not uncommon to see members dressed much less formally. Some clubs have gone so far as to allow members to wear jeans (although some are still debating this issue). Some clubs allow jeans but draw the line at tattered or 'distressed' jeans.

Clubs have also relaxed their dress codes on golf courses and tennis courts, although the default is often a collared short and tee shirts are still frowned upon. There may also be restrictions on athletic wear in certain parts of the club, and where (and how) hats may be worn. However, overall, dress codes are not as restrictive as they were a generation ago. This particular trend is seems more apparent in the USA though, as many clubs in Commonwealth countries have maintained more traditional dress codes.

The trends toward casualness also affects the look and feel of the interiors of clubhouses, which have come to more resemble informal living spaces. It also involves relaxing some long-held social traditions, such as how acquaintances address each other. In the end, casualization has affected clubs in many ways, beyond just how people dress.

Even though the discussion above is an accurate portrayal of the changes taking place in clubs, we must take the 'Professor's Prerogative' and share our views on students visiting clubs. Students should always remember that when they visit a club (for a class project, a field trip, or a meeting), they are a guest of the club. Further, on their visits, students are representing their class (or club), their college or university and their professor. In our classes, we always have two rules that we insist students observe: (1) cell phones are to be turned off and out of reach; and (2) students are to dress professionally. We have never been sorry to have these rules – even in cases where the students have been better dressed than our hosts!

Recreation

We know that time availability, cost and level of interest are all affecting the range of recreational activities in clubs. We have seen that because of the combination of these factors, golf is less popular that it once was – in certain regions and at some clubs. But the trend here is that clubs are looking for new and interesting ways for its members to engage in golf (as well as other activities). At a recent CMAA World Conference, a club with a progressive golf programme was profiled. At that particular club, the golf professionals get out of the office and/or the pro shop and spend the majority of their time giving impromptu lessons to their members. The pros meet and greet golfers at the tee to give advice on technique.

This accomplishes a variety of things. It gives the member a sense of importance due to the attention that they receive, however briefly. It also improves their game, which increases their passion for the game. Finally, the lessons are free, adding to a sense of value for the member. Other clubs are trying similar strategies.

It is important to note that while growth in golf has leveled off, other sports and recreational activities have stepped up to take its place including a variety of racquet sports, aquatics, bocce, and badminton.

Other clubs are trying to engage different demographic groups as well. According to *Club and Resort Business* magazine,

> *"Superstition Mountain Golf & Country Club in Gold Canyon, Ariz., and the Golf Club of Estrella in Goodyear, Ariz., are among the golf properties attempting to attract children, families, women and friends of regular golfers through activities such as croquet tournaments, craft-beer tasting events, and free equipment rentals for children..."The key question is how do we engage Millennials and the next generation," said Mark Gurnow, General Manager of Superstition Mountain Golf & Country Club in Gold Canyon, Ariz. "We're constantly looking at ways to make it more fun."*

https://clubandresortbusiness.com/2018/02/arizona-golf-facilities-focus -fun-broaden-appeal/.

A recent report by the Bureau of Labor Statistics (USA) looked at the primary forms of exercise that Americans (aged 15 and older) engaged in. Top activities included walking, weight lifting, cardiovascular, running and water sports such as swimming. Golf was listed at number 7 (www.bls.gov/spotlight/2017/sports-and-exercise/pdf/sports-and-exercise.pdf). The report makes it clear that the popularity of different activities varies among genders and age groups, something that clubs are well aware of.

Expect to see clubs continue to diversify the range of recreational activities to engage different demographic groups, particularly children. One club, Bluejack National in Texas (as profiled in *Club Management* magazine), has an area called The Fort, which includes water slides and splashpads, a wiffle ball park, zip lines, and a ropes course, among other things.

But perhaps the athletic activity that has capitalized most on members' shifting interests, is the general area of fitness, including aerobics, strength training, and cross training. As discussed in Chapter 7, this is where many clubs are investing in facilities, equipment and people. Fitness, as a hobby, would seem to be in the right place at the right time as society becomes more health conscious. It also cuts across demographic groups (based on age and gender). Finally, it does not require the time commitment that other activities require. Just witness the attention being given to the '7 minute workout'. To be effective though, clubs need to find ways to personalize the fitness experience for members while, at the same time, offering classes, to provide the social experience.

Food and beverage

In addition to recreation, food and beverage is one of the focal points of clubs. Clubs have always been challenged by food and beverage, trying to find the proper balance between members who want the same familiar offerings with members wanting variety. More and more clubs seem to be finding this balance in their menus, while offering their dining in more comfortable and more casual settings. One could easily identify the entire food and beverage area as a trend, as clubs renovate dining areas, upgrade bars, increase outdoor seating capacity, differentiate their beverage lists and diversify menus. In short, we can declare with confidence that club dining is much more exciting and innovative than it has been in a long time. Some of these changes have been driven by members who dine out in trendy restaurants and travel more than previous generations, and want samplings of those experiences at their own clubs. Thus, as one example, the fusion concept (blending of different cuisines) has been introduced in many clubs.

In some ways, the demands that members have made in the area of food and beverage are greater than the demands made elsewhere in the club. Food and beverage has literally been turned upside down and sideways when one considers how much it has changed in the last 10 years. While the dining spaces have changed (table settings, lighting, seating, table configurations) and dining has become more casual and changed to invite a greater degree of social interaction, the biggest change that has occurred has been with the food and beverages, themselves. Many of the same trends that we are seeing in restaurants are apparent in clubs: farm to table products, healthy options, upscale beverages and craft/boutique products. Clubs are also seeing differences in preferences among demographic groups. In what can only be described as a role reversal, we are seeing younger members re-establishing a cocktail culture while older members are rediscovering premium wines by the glass and microbrews.

Perhaps these changes are best exemplified by how wine is now being treated in clubs. Trevor Noonan, CCM, CCE, the COO of Toronto Club, in downtown Toronto, shares his members' enthusiasm for wine. The club, with an inventory of 15,000 bottles, takes a three pronged approach to its wine programme. First, it hosts four high-end wine events each year, each with a different theme. One is the 'Chairman's Wine Dinner' in which the chairman of the wine committee is given access to the wine cellar and tasked with choosing wines and a theme for the black-tie dinner. A recent event focused on classified growths of Bordeaux. Because of the quality of the events, all of the wine events are fully-subscribed.

The second piece of their program is a series of classes held throughout the year entitled 'Wine 101', specifically designed for members who are not thoroughly versed in wine. Classes take a '10,000 foot view' of a region, grape or vintage and include tastings, talks and visits with wine industry professionals.

Finally, the club, by special authority from the provincial liquor commission, is not only a licensee but also an agent, which allows it to import its own wine which is exclusive to the club. It does this once a year from a specific country (or region) and is able to make the wine available to it members to take home for their own cellars.

Another wine trend sees more clubs hiring sommeliers or even combining the role of sommelier with beverage director. A club in metropolitan New York was one of the first in the region to employ its own sommelier. Karen Collazo (WSET Level 3), Beverage Services Manager and Sommelier, described the wine programme at her club as having an extensive bottle selection which is supported by regular wine programming throughout the year. The club offers over 100 different bottles of wine, of which 20 are offered by the glass. While there is a wine focus throughout the entire club, a core group of members belong to a wine club within the club. These 70 members pay a fee to be able to participate in private tastings, attend other wine events, and meet visiting winemakers – all organized by Karen. Members are also able to buy wine through the club, and store it in wine lockers.

Clay Wheeler, also a SWET Level 3, is the Dining Room Manager and Sommelier/ Beverage Director at the Argyle Club, an historic dining club in Texas. He has compiled an impressive wine list that includes wine by the bottle and by the glass. In addition to his regular wines by the glass list, he also offers members a 'Sommelier Select' list which includes wines that he feels are a good value as well as wines that members might not try otherwise. By offering them this list, members are able to order wines that they might not normally order by the bottle, such as grand cru champagnes. The club has a *Coravin*™ wine system so that the wine is preserved between servings. In addition to daily wine service, Clay also organizes six events each year for the club's wine society. The events are theme based and are described as having an educational component. A recent event profiled rose wines from Provence. In addition, he also puts together four wine dinners each year, where the menu is paired with high-end wines. Finally, the club has also worked with Clubster to develop a wine function for the club app. Clay is able to post wine notes, announcements and other wine related information through the app for interested members.

Finally, Natalie Sailer, Senior Assistant Manager and Sommelier at the Chevy Chase Club, outside of Washington DC, handles all wine and beverages for the Winter Center, the club's largest casual dining facility. She has observed an over 100 % increase in sales of bottles over the last year. They have over 150 wines on offer which includes a '50 under 50' list where all of the bottles are priced under $50 USD. They are also riding the rosé craze by offering a separate list of rosés from around the world and rosé and food pairings. They also have robust beer sales and have seen an increase in both rum and vodka based drinks.

In sum, one of us can recall the time when offering premium wines by the glass at a club was a novelty but has now come to be expected. Times have changed!

Families

The history of how the extended family was treated at clubs is an interesting one. If one goes back long enough, women and children were typically not welcome at many clubs and, if so, only in specific areas and only at specific times. This has all changed spectacularly though at most clubs, which have gone so far as to: develop additional membership categories to better accommodate families, eliminated discriminatory policies (such as days and times when women could golf) and added programmes and services for women, and children of various ages. Some of this is old news. However, the pace of accommodation seems to be accelerating as more clubs try to become family-centric. For some, it simply meant a change of policy. For others, it meant reconfiguring space in the clubhouse. And for others, it means offering amenities that were once thought to be too obtuse. Now, it is not uncommon to see camps, sports clinics, exercise classes for women, and child-care. Yoga, Pilates and boot camp are offered, as are spa/massage services and mixers (such as yoga and wine) of all kinds. In an article from *Club Management* magazine (2017), Rob DeMore, senior vice-president of operations for Troon Privé is quoted as saying, "Offering something for everyone in the family, from the 3-year-old child to the grandparent is the primary factor for attracting membership at clubs today." Not much more needs to be said about this other than the more clubs can embrace the family, the more likely the entire family is to remain members.

Reciprocal agreements

Reciprocal agreements are formal agreements between clubs which allow members of one club to use the services of the other club, generally for a fee and with restrictions. They have existed for as long as clubs have, but we include them here because it seems that managers are rediscovering the power of these agreements. They offer a value added benefit to members with virtually no additional marginal costs to the club. For the price of joining a single club, members have the benefit of being able to use others, sometimes hundreds of others. This is especially advantageous to members who travel frequently and are able to use facilities on the road. City clubs with reciprocal agreements offer the added benefit of being able to stay in overnight guest rooms of their reciprocal clubs.

Such agreements also offer other potential benefits. If a club is undergoing extensive renovations on the golf course or in the clubhouse, and portions of the club must be closed down, some agreements allow members to have privileges at other nearby clubs during the renovation period.

Yacht clubs have developed reciprocal agreements to a near art form – members of one club are able to sail from one club to another and have docking or mooring privileges, or stay in guest rooms if available.

Companies such as ClubCorp, have capitalized on the concept where it allows its members to use the services of its network of 300 (owned or affiliated) clubs.

Aside from the ability to use another club when travelling or when one's host club is undergoing renovations, reciprocal agreements allow clubs (and their members) to develop stronger relationships with one another, allow members occasional diversions, can increase revenues and can even result in additional memberships.

An article in *Golf Course Industry* magazine sums up the benefits of reciprocal agreements well, "If structured properly, reciprocal playing privileges offer a great value proposition to the members, increase the traffic on the golf course and in the clubhouse and also substantially increase the revenues of the club. In order to provide some degree of protection to the members and their families, reciprocal privilege holders generally are subject to certain restrictions on tee times and usage of the golf course and related facilities." (www.golfcourseindustry.com/article/gci-080811-private-clubs-new -world-order/)

Technology

We have long said that clubs were laggards when it comes to embracing technology. This too is changing. Technology is now having an impact on every aspect of club operations. Something that began with (and was limited to) back-of-the-house accounting functions has moved beyond the office space into the member sphere. As managers, staff, and members become more comfortable with technology (and, particularly digital technology and social media), clubs are able to leverage current technologies to both improve services and, in some cases, reduce costs.

An article by Michael Zisman, in *Club Director* (Summer 2015), identifies what he calls 'enterprise architecture', which has four primary areas: member facing systems (which includes a club's website and reservation capabilities); back end systems (financial systems and POS, etc.); infrastrucure systems (including security); and member owned technology (cell phones, etc.).

Examples of tech applications in clubs are almost too numerous to mention but in recent years, clubs have transitioned their newsletters from hard-copy to digital (as part of expanding e-communications), allowed members to make tee-times on-line, and developed more interactive, and powerful, websites. But perhaps the greatest development has been the ability for clubs to develop their own apps which allow members to access every function they need from their smartphones. Now members can use their apps to make reservations, register for events and access the club calendar. The club can also use the apps as a means of issuing push notifications.

Companies, such as Jonas and Clubessential (and their affiliates), began by offering back-of-the-house software for clubs and are now offering an entire suite of services from web site development to reservation systems to apps and membership management systems.

We should also mention social media at this point. For many years, clubs were reluctant to adopt social media, largely due to concerns over the privacy of their members. But clubs have begun to recognize that social media platforms, such as Facebook, Twitter and Instagram, can help engage members and strengthen the club community. More and more clubs are hiring communications directors, or even IT teams, to look after their social media programmes. Further, companies such as MembersFirst, can provide professional expertise in establishing a presence on these platforms. Clubs have found that engaging with members on social media can bring benefits as well as allowing clubs to be part of the conversation.

Clubs can also create groups within the club, for members with specific interests. For for-profit clubs, social media can serve as an additional means of marketing for special events and new members.

Social media brings a downside. Among other things, clubs are cautioned to create private spaces to avoid public exposure. Further, member feedback can be more immediate, and more public, necessitating a quick management response.

Governance

While governance, per se, is not a trend, the ways in which club managers are viewing and tweaking the governance model is changing. Three major changes are taking place in the area of governance. First, the role of the traditional general manager is expanding, beyond simply looking after day to day management of the club. Their roles are becoming broader with more responsibility, that used to be reserved for boards of directors. In short, they are becoming more active participants with boards, particularly in the areas of capital planning, strategic planning and financial management.

Second, as the role of general managers changes, more of an effort is being made to more clearly delineate the responsibilities of board members (both individually and collectively) and the general manager and his or her professional staff. Several commentators have noted that high functioning clubs have high functioning boards, which are defined by knowing what their roles are. Because, or as a result of this, the Club Management Association of America (CMAA) often includes board members in their governance workshops, in an effort to better educate board members and improve communications between boards and managers.

Finally, the ways in which boards are elected and the way that new board members are indoctrinated is changing. More and more board elections are 'uncontested', meaning that board members are not running against each other, and instead, agreements about who will run for which positions are decided before votes are even held. This reduces animosity and can allow for more effective planning. Along the same lines, clubs, and boards, are making more of an effort to provide adequate orientation and training for new members, which is important, especially if terms are relatively short (two years or less). An emerging term is 'onboarding' which refers to effective welcoming of new members. The same term can be applied to the process of welcoming, and preparing new board members. With good succession planning for various board and committee positions, this becomes easier.

The Club Management Association of America (www.cmaa.org) must receive credit for much of the work they are doing on behalf of clubs and club managers. Their Governance/Leadership summits have been very effective in bringing board members and general managers together to explore best practices in governance. Recent summits have covered such topics as roles and responsibilities of the board, board self-evaluation, and data driven decision making.

Finally, there are many services and resources available for clubs to help them create more functional boards. ClubBenchmarking often makes presentations to boards; there is a magazine for board members entitled *Boardroom Magazine;* and some companies such as Club Board Professionals, specialize in offering solutions to clubs in the area of governance.

Capital projects

More clubs are undergoing capital projects than ever before, primarily involving aging clubhouses. A look at clubhouse projects just a few years ago indicated clubs were spending an average of about $3 million to upgrade their facilities. We know of several projects that have been completed in recent years which required investments of $20 million or more. Today, general managers must combine political and financial skills, along with being general contractors.

A recent example of a club undertaking a major renovation is the Harvard Club of Boston, a club with two facilities in Boston that was founded in 1908. They recently underwent a $16 million USD renovation in their main clubhouse to improve several areas of the clubhouse, including the dining areas. Improvements were also made to the front-of-the-house areas such as the foyer and front desk. Also, a new private dining area was added and several new guest rooms were brought on-line. Planning began in 2013 and construction began in 2015, being completed in 2016. A good portion of the funding came from the sale of an upper portion of the building's annex to a developer. General Manager Stephen Cummings, CCM, CCE, oversaw the entire project. The completed project is expected to increase current member satisfaction while acting as an attraction for potential members.

Clubs are turning more of their attention to major projects for two primary reasons. First, many clubs, particularly those which occupy clubhouses built in the 1960s or earlier, are in need of a refresh or even more. Second, clubs are realizing that their clubs cannot afford to look dated when trying to attract newer, and younger, managers.

There is also additional expertise and support for clubs looking to undergo capital projects. For instance, companies can provide expertise for every stage of a project from capital reserve analyses to conceptualization to architectural planning and design.

Greening of the industry

As is true with other segments of the hospitality industry, the club industry has made efforts to make its operations greener and more sustainable. Clubs of all kinds – city clubs, country clubs and yacht clubs – have environmental impacts. Aside from demands from communities and members for them to be better environmental stewards, legislation is also driving some of these changes. As more municipalities suffer from drought (for instance in the western USA, New South Wales in Australia, Israel and South Africa, among others) laws are being introduced which restrict water usage. This has a disproportionate impact on golf clubs.

In Cape Town, SA, the city has imposed severe restrictions as it approaches 'Day Zero'. Two restrictions pertaining to clubs state that: "No watering/irrigation with municipal drinking water allowed. This includes watering/irrigation of gardens, vegetables, agricultural crops, sports fields, golf courses, nurseries, parks and other open spaces. Nurseries and customers involved in agricultural activities or with historical gardens may apply for exemption," and "All non-residential properties (e.g. commercial and industrial properties, schools, clubs and institutions) must ensure that their monthly consumption of municipal drinking water is reduced by 45% compared to the corresponding period in 2015 (pre-drought)." Clubs in drought stricken parts of the world are getting creative in finding alternative sources of water for irrigation, including, using brown water, creating irrigation ponds and using smart sprinkler systems.

In the USA, the USGA has proposed that courses take a series of actions in an attempt to limit water use:

- "Using recycled water, which reduces reliance on potable water for irrigation.
- Having a well-designed and properly maintained irrigation system that applies water as efficiently as possible with little waste.
- Use of water saving devices, such as moisture meters and in-ground sensors to measure and report soil moisture levels so that intelligent irrigation programing decisions can be made.
- Employing proper aeration and soil cultivation programs so that any water applied infiltrates the soil and is not lost to run-off.
- Reducing turf in out of play areas where turf is not necessary.

- Root pruning trees near critical turf areas to reduce the competition for water between trees and turf.
- Use of mulch below trees and in landscape beds.
- Addressing indoor water use with water-efficient toilets and fixtures.
- Education and training of maintenance personnel on the importance of proper water application techniques and using water as efficiently as possible."

(http://www.usga.org/course-care/water-resource-center/how-can-courses-minimize-water.html).

Also, golf clubs can work with Audubon International (a conservation and education nonprofit organization) to help preserve natural areas. In an article from *Grounds Maintenance*, Katherine Woodford describes the program: "With the support of the USGA, in 1991 International Audubon initiated the Audubon Cooperative Sanctuary Program for Golf Courses. Today in the United States, 354 courses have met the requirements to receive designation as Certified Audubon Cooperative Sanctuaries."

Another group, the GEO Foundation,based in Scotland, is a sustainability movement focusing on golf courses. They are "An international golf community and industry that is:

- Protecting and fostering biodiversity and natural landscapes
- Using natural resources responsibly
- Generating positive social and economic value
- Earning recognition and trust as a sustainable sport and leader
- Using its reach to raise awareness for sustainability in wider world"

(www.sustainable.golf)

Environmentalism, or sustainability can take many other forms aside from land and water preservation and conservation. In an excellent article in *Club Management* magazine (Summer 2015) entitled 'The Business Case for Sustainability', multiple examples of clubs are given that are trying to manage their waste stream, designing clubhouses that are LEED certified, and limiting (or recycling) water used for irrigating golf courses. The Army Navy Country Club (with two facilities in Virginia) was recognized for its new clubhouse in Arlington, Virginia with LEED Silver certification for meeting LEED standards. The certification is based on construction, space utilization and resource efficiency, among other factors, in looking at the total environmental impact.

Finally, in a different sector of the club industry, the RYA (Royal Yachting Association, which is the boating authority in the UK), and The Green Blue, their environmental initiative, provides recommendations and guidelines around a variety of boating practices including anchoring, best practices with fuel and oil, cleaning of boats, and resource efficiency. Their statement on marine waste reads as follows:

"Marine litter has a major impact on wildlife, the main issues being entanglement and ingestion. It is estimated that over 50,000 marine mammals die every year from becoming tangled in or eating marine litter. Plastics are the most prevalent beach litter material. Certain types of plastics are known to absorb chemicals from the surrounding environment, such as PCBs and heavy metals at concentrations up to 1 million times higher than in waters around them. The ingestion of these toxins can have life threatening impacts upon marine wildlife. Research shows that little of the litter entering the marine environment comes from marine boating; the 2007 MCS beach watch survey identified the main contributers as beach visitors (35.3%) and the fishing industry (13.7%). However boaters are likely to be more aware of litter than other groups and should still do their part to prevent any litter from entering the water."

(www.thegreenblue.org.uk)

Summary

These are not the only trends affecting clubs. Others include labour shortages in some markets, changes in the supply chain, changing legislation, marketing and membership, clubhouse design, changes in leasehold arrangements (such as in Hong Kong), and trends in ownership. We have tried to summarize the ones that we feel are most immediate and far reaching.

Discussion questions

1   What are the major recreational activities in your area? Are they well represented at clubs? Could the clubs with which you are familiar benefit by introducing a greater diversity of activities? What would be the challenges of doing so?

2   What are some of the trends that you are observing in commercial restaurants? How many of these trends, if any, do you see reflected in club dining?

3 What are some additional trends that you have observed, and are not discussed here. What factors do you think are driving those trends?

References

Andruss, P. (2015) 'The Business Case for Sustainability', *Club Management*, Summer.

Bureau of Labor Statistics (2017), www.bls.gov/spotlight/2017/sports-and-exercise/pdf/sports-and-exercise.pdf

Carter, K. (2017) State of the private club, *Club Management*, March/April.

Club and Resort Business, (2018) https://clubandresortbusiness.com/2018/02/arizona-golf-facilities-focus-fun-broaden-appeal/

Golf Course Industry Magazine, (2018) http://www.golfcourseindustry.com/article/gci-080811-private-clubs-new-world-order/

RYA (2018), www.thegreenblue.org.uk

United States Golf Association, www.usga.org/course-care/water-resource-center/how-can-courses-minimize-water.html

Zisman, M (2015), Taking on tech, *Club Director*, **33**(3), 14-19.

Bibliography

Allison, B.R. (1986), *The Rockaway Hunting Club*, Alan Brown, Inc., Brattleboro, VT.

Angel, J.R. (1988), *The Australian Club 1838 – 1988: The first 150 years*, The Australian Club, Sydney.

Baltzell, E.D. (1958), *Philadelphia Gentlemen: The making of a national upper class*, The Free Press, Glencoe, IL.

Becker, H. & Pearson, R. (1979), *The Jewish Community of Hartford, Connecticut, 1880-1929*. www.AmericanJewishArchives.org.

Behrend, J. & Lewis, P.N. (1998), *Challenges and Champions: The Royal and Ancient Golf Club, 1754 – 1883*, The Royal & Ancient Golf Club of St. Andrews, Scotland.

Bourke, A. (1892), *The History of White's*, Bourke, London.

Cannon, R. (1975), *Brief History of the Savannah Golf Club*, Self Published.

Chambers, G. & Roulston, W. (2009, *The Ulster Reform Club, past and present*, Ulster Reform Club and Ulster Historical Society, Belfast.

Chambers, M. (1996), *The Unplayable Lie: The untold story of women and discrimination in American golf*, Pocket Books, New York.

Chaster, A.W. (1903), *Wertheimer's law relating to clubs*, Stevens and Haynes, Temple Bar.

Chenery, W.L. (1955), *The University Club: Yesterday and today*, The University Club, NY.

Collard, E.A. (1957), *The Saint James's Club: The story of the beginnings of the Saint James's Club*, Saint James's Club, Montreal.

Clubs and Resort Business (n.d.), https://clubandresortbusiness.com.

CMAA (2012) *Uniform System of Financial Reporting for Clubs*, CMAA, Alexandria, VA.

deServille, P. (2003), *3 Barrack Street: The Weld Club, 1871 – 2001*, The Helicon Press Pty Ltd, Wahroonga, NSW.

Fairfield, F.G. (1893), *The clubs of New York*, Henry L. Hinton, New York.

Forbes, A. (1942), *Early Myopia*. Forbes, Hamilton, MA.

Glanz, R. (1969), 'The rise of the Jewish Club in America', *Jewish Social Studies*, **31**(2), 82-99.

Graves, C. (1964), *Leather Armchairs: The book of London clubs*, Coward-McCann, New York.

Gray, M.W. (1987), *The Edgewood Club of Tivoli*, Edgewood Club, New York.

Halbfinger, D. (2003), 'Golf: Public and private distinctions,' *New York Times*, 10 April.

Hirsch, L.A. (2016), *Golf Property Analysis and Valuation*. Appraisal Institute, Chicago.

Holton, L. (2008), *For Members Only: A history and guide to Chicago's oldest private clubs*. Lake Claremont Press, Chicago.

Jolly-Ryan, J. (2006), 'Teed off about private club discrimination on the taxpayer's dime: Tax exemptions and other government privileges to discriminatory private clubs,' *William and Mary Journal of Women and the Law*, **3**(1) 235-272.

Kendall, D. (2008), *Members Only*. Rowman & Littlefield: Lanham, MD.

Leigh, E.C.A. (1907), *A List of English clubs*, Spottiswoode, London.

Lejeune, A. (1993), *White's: The first three hundred years*. A & C Black, London.

Levine, P. (1995). 'The American Hebrew looks at "Our Crowd": The Jewish country club in the 1920s', *American Jewish History*, **83**(1) 27 – 49.

Lippincott, H.A. (1954), *A History of the Philadelphia Cricket Club: 1854 – 1954*, Philadelphia Cricket Club, Philadelphia.

Mayo, J. (1998), *The American Country Club: its origins and development.* Rutgers University Press, New Jersey.

McBurney, M. (2003), *The Great Adventure: 100 years at the Arts & Letters Club.* The Arts & Letters Club, Toronto.

McNicoll, R (1988), *Number 36 Collins Street.* Lee Printing, Singapore.

Merritt, P (1915), The Club of Odd Volumes, *Bibliographic Society of America*, **9**(1), 21-34.

Moss, RJ (2001), *Golf and the American Country Club,* University of Illinois, Urbana, IL.

National Club Association (2013) *HR Management: Best Practices for Private Clubs*, NCA: Washington DC.

National Club Association (2010), *The Legal Reference Guide for Private Clubs*, NCA: Washington DC.

Ouzounian, R. (2005), *The Boulevard Club: 100 years on the shore,* McArthur, Toronto.

Perdue, J. & Koenigsfeld, J. (Eds.) (2013), *Contemporary Club Management*, Educational Institute, Lansing, Michigan.

Pixley, F.W. (1914), *Clubs and their Management*, Pitman and Sons, Ltd., London.

Probert, H. (2004), *128: The Story of the Royal Air Force Club,* Royal Air Force Club, London.

Rossiter, J.H. (1901), *Club Men of New York*, Self-published, New York.

Schmidgall, R..S & Damito, J.W. (2001), *Accounting for Club Operations*, Educational Institute,Lansing, Michigan.

Sheppard, S.T. (1916), *The Byculla Club.* Bennet Coleman & Co., Bombay.

Shipnik, A. (2004), *The Battle for Augusta National*, Simon and Schuster, NY.

Simmons, M. (1986), *Union Club of the City of New York*, Union Club, New York.

Stump, M. (2018), *Club Tax*, Mitchell Stump, Palm Beach Gardens, FL.

Stump, M. (2018), *It's All about Golf*, Mitchell Stump, Palm Beach Gardens, FL.

Royal Montreal Golf Club (1973) *The Royal Montreal Golf Club 1873 – 1973: The Centennial of Golf in North America*, Royal Montreal Golf Club, Montreal.

Tringali, J.A. (2003), *Yachting Customs and Courtesies,* Calkins Harbor Publishing Company, Florida.

Whitelaw, R.O. (1978), *The History of the University Club of St. Louis: 1872 – 1978*, University Club of St. Louis, St. Louis.

Williams, A.W. (1979), *A Social History of the Greater Boston clubs*, Barre Publishing, Boston.

Williams, A.W. (1969), *Social History of the Club of Odd Volumes 1887 – 1967*, Boston, The Club of Odd Volumes.

Wister, O. (1934), *The Philadelphia Club: 1834 – 1934.* The Philadelphia Club, Philadelphia.

Wolfe, R.P. (2011), *The New Orleans Lawn Tennis Club: Oldest in the Americas.* Multi-Media Technology Group, South Korea.

Index

Printed in the United States
By Bookmasters